MW01203897

A BRIEF INTRODUCTION TO A PHILOSOPHY OF MUSIC AND MUSIC EDUCATION AS SOCIAL PRAXIS

A Brief Introduction to a Philosophy of Music and Music Education as Social Praxis presents a *praxial theory* of music education, as defined by the author. This introduction to a *contemporary* philosophy of music education is based on a variety of scholarly sources and is grounded in an interdisciplinary approach, for undergraduate and graduate students in music education. Drawing upon scholarship from a range of disciplines, including philosophy and sociology, the book emphasizes and highlights how to think of music as an active social practice and offers an alternative to existing approaches to music education.

A Brief Introduction to a Philosophy of Music and Music Education as Social Praxis supplements Foundations or Methods courses in the Music Education curriculum. The short chapters facilitate use as complementary assigned reading, for discussion, assignments, and other applications according to the course focus.

Thomas A. Regelski, Ph.D., is a "Distinguished Professor" (Emeritus) of the State University of New York (SUNY), Fredonia. He is also Docent of Helsinki University.

A BRIEF INTRODUCTION TO A PHILOSOPHY OF MUSIC AND MUSIC EDUCATION AS SOCIAL PRAXIS

Thomas A. Regelski, Ph.D.

School of Music, SUNY Fredonia, NY, USA (Emeritus)
Docent, Helsinki University (Finland)

Routledge
Taylor & Francis Group

NEW YORK AND LONDON

First published 2016
by Routledge
711 Third Avenue, New York, NY 10017

and by Routledge
2 Park Square, Milton Park, Abingdon, Oxon, OX14 4RN

*Routledge is an imprint of the Taylor & Francis Group,
an informa business*

© 2016 Taylor & Francis

Library of Congress Cataloging-in-Publication Data
Regelski, Thomas A., 1941– author.
Musica practica : a brief introduction to music and music education
philosophy as social praxis / Thomas A. Regelski, Ph.D.
pages cm
Includes bibliographical references.
1. Music—Instruction and study—Philosophy.   2. School music—
Instruction and study—Philosophy.   3. Music and philosophy.
I. Title.
MT1.R417 2016
780.71—dc23   2015022073

ISBN: 978-1-138-92123-8 (hbk)
ISBN: 978-1-138-92124-5 (pbk)
ISBN: 978-1-315-68649-3 (ebk)

Typeset in Times New Roman
by Apex CoVantage, LLC

Senior Editor: Constance Ditzel
Senior Editorial Assistant: Aurora Montgomery
Production Editor: Katie Hemmings
Marketing Manager: Jessica Plummer

I dedicate this book to my MayDay Group colleagues,
who have been both supportive and informative
over the years.
Helsinki, May 2015

CONTENTS

CHAPTER OVERVIEW

Philosophy seeks to identify confused thinking and action, making action more intelligent, more informed, more congruent with responsibly held, defensible beliefs.

Wayne D. Bowman and Ana Lucía Frega, eds.,
*The Oxford Handbook of Philosophy in
Music Education*, 2012, 5

The double-edged role for philosophy described in the philosophical action ideal guiding this monograph promotes its organization into two parts. Part One is an *ideology critique* of and challenge to the "confused thinking" of the aesthetic rationale for music education. Then in Part Two, "Theory into Praxis," beliefs "more informed" by scholarship often ignored in music education circles are proposed as alternatives for "responsibly held" and "defensible" teaching actions. This organization follows the spirit of "critical philosophy" (of Kant) and the usual Critical Theory methodology of a critique followed by positive alternatives. "Action," here, is understood as *praxis*, the typical translation of this Greek/Latin philosophical term.

Reading the following overviews before and after reading each section may be useful.

PART ONE—IDEOLOGY CRITIQUE

"Identifying Confused Thinking and Actions" behind Taken-for-Granted Aesthetic Assumptions

Introduction

Aesthetic Theory and the Spectatorship/ Connoisseurship Theory of 'Fine Art'

The aesthetic benefit of music taken for granted by many music teachers as the rationale for their curricular programs is entirely speculative in its origins.

Aestheticians vary so widely in their theoretical accounts that aesthetics provides no stable basis for music education. Yet the aesthetic ideology is influential despite music educators' lack of background in aesthetics.

Praxis and "Practice Theory"

The social history of music and the insights provided by contemporary "practice theory" in social philosophy situate music as a major source of human sociality. Praxis, in the sense described here, provides ample empirical evidence, not speculations, as to the importance of music to society and culture and its proper role in school.

Chapter One: Musica Practica[1] Compared to Aesthetic Speculations

The Invention of 'Fine Art'—from Aisthesis to Aesthetics

Music was thoroughly praxial for thousands of years until, in the mid-eighteenth century, the rise of aesthetic theories in philosophy, socially motivated, led to its departure from earlier bases in what the Greeks called "*aisthesis*," the bodily source of sensible experience and knowledge. Music (i.e., 'high' music) was thereafter placed on a pedestal that reflected or even created social class differences along musical lines. These differences still exist and are problematic for music teachers today.

Autonomous Music as Divorced from Everyday Life

Common to neo-Kantian aesthetic theories is the extolling of music's autonomy as separate and 'above' everyday life. Claims of "art for art's sake" thus relegated music to rare occasions of leisure and greatly limited the many social values of music. However, the social bases of these theories are ignored, and 'good music' is said to be above mundane social meanings.

---

1 For a detailed exposition of this Latin term and its vast implications for the present study, see Michael Chanan, *Musica Practica: The Social Practice of Western Music from Gregorian Chant to Postmodernism* (New York: Verso, 1994). "Community is the meeting place of different voices talking together, exchanging and debating experience and knowledge. Music is one of the instruments of this process, a means of social intercourse, and like all art-forms a vehicle of expression both individual and social" (38).The present monograph is indebted to the social praxis of music described in Chanan's socio-musical study. "Musica practica" should not be confused with the "practica musica"® ear-training software, although the latter is clearly praxial in intent (although its claims to "common practice" are limited to tonal musics that no longer comport with modern musical life).

Kant and 'Taste for Beauty'

Emmanuel Kant's theories about "free" beauty were *mistakenly* generalized by subsequent philosophers into a *theory of art* and 'good taste' that led to the connoisseurship premises of 'good music' that make music seem to have appeared from Mars. This false theory of art and music leads inevitably to a *social class* distinction between being musically 'cultivated' and having only a lower-class, common sensibility (aisthesis).

The Ascendancy of Presentational Music over Participatory Musics

Aesthetic theories led quickly to music for public concerts and recitals. And music education, especially in university music schools and conservatories, has regularly ignored the preponderance of participatory musics in the world in favor of Western presentational (concert) traditions. This prejudice is inherited by school music; even when participatory musics are (rarely) included, the focus tends to be on the next concert, not on inspiring a disposition for lifelong involvement.

Chapter Two: *Obscurum per obscurius*

Aesthetic This and That

Aesthetic theories *obscure* the natural appeal of music. Their attempts to rationalize beauty and like-minded concepts only further obfuscate the all-too-evident attraction that musics of all kinds have for people. Aesthetic rationales are not needed to explain the appeal of music to people—for example, to children.

Autonomania

The separation of art and music from the practical, personal, and social world of everyday life is a unique consequence of the aestheticized philosophy of art and music found in Western culture. It relegates music to contemplation, thoroughly ignores the many social and praxial uses and functions of music throughout the world, and discounts its daily role in the lives of most people, even in Western societies.

The Sacralization of Music

Aesthetic values are articulated to sound nobly like solemn religious, ethical, and intellectual ideals and have led to a quasi-religious role for 'fine' art and music. High-minded rhetoric about the almost mystical, spiritual nature accorded to aesthetic experience is credited with replacing the religious dimension of life that was shunted aside in Western history by the eighteenth-century promotion of reason and science. "Popular" musics are thus a kind of sacrilege to aesthetes.

What Is the Value of School Music?

Since music of all kinds is an absolutely central feature of contemporary life, we don't need aesthetic speculations about the value of teaching music. Its many social values are right before our eyes and ears.

Chapter Three: Predictable Problems of Aesthetic Theory as a Basis for Music Education

Aesthetic Metaphysics as Premises for Music Education

The sacralized metaphysics of aesthetic theories (there are many theories) are pragmatically unsuited to meeting the usual instructional responsibilities and challenges faced by teachers in schools. Thus, many everyday practical problems are created on the basis of unstated, selective, and idiosyncratic aesthetic *sloganeering* by teachers.

The Disinterested Aesthetic Attitude

The "disinterested" *aesthetic attitude* said to be a condition for aesthetic experience is obviously difficult to teach, inspire, or encourage formally in a school subject. Students who are disinterested in their other studies are not disinterested in 'their' musics. Music education that intends to *convert* students to the quasi-sacred premises of musical autonomy advanced by aesthetic theories is wrongheaded and dysfunctional.

Intangibility of Aesthetic Improvement

The inner, personal nature claimed for aesthetic responding makes aesthetic theory an ineffective basis for objectively planning or evaluating teaching or learning. Moreover, easily made but unsupportable claims about aesthetically educating students' *tastes* are not supported by their actual musical choices in later life.

Legitimation and Advocacy

The vagueness and intangibility of aesthetic rationales for music education have led to a "legitimation crisis" for school music. Such crises arise when claims made by a social institution are not met in actuality. Thus, attempts to legitimate claims about the relevance of the institution of school music result in advocacy, advertising, and propaganda. The mounting social challenge to the existence of school music is evidence of its worsening legitimation crisis.

Music Education as a Conserving Activity

Music education rests on educational policy divided between the ideals of *transmission* and *transformation*. Thus, it seeks both to conserve and transmit the gains of musical praxis from the past *and* the intention to transform graduates and society to comfortable lives in the present and future. Overemphasis on the conserving ideal breeds a museum-like role for music rather than a living musical culture that can transform people's lives.

Music Education versus the Aesthetic Ideology

Music teachers who rely heavily on the vagueness of speculative aesthetic claims typically fail to notice that their teaching has not amounted to an effective *music* education, one that makes a notable, lasting, and pragmatic *musical* difference in students' musical lives, dispositions, tastes, and choices. Claims for the aesthetic benefits of school music fall on the 'deaf ears' of students (and adults) for whom music is praxial.

The Bottom Line

Understanding both music and teaching as social praxis promotes musical growth in graduates that overcomes the many problems created by the vagueness of the aesthetic rationale and its ideology for school music. In a praxial model, the benefits of music education are seen *empirically* in the difference music makes in people's lives.

PART TWO—THEORY INTO PRAXIS AND PRAXIS INFORMED BY THEORY

. . . making action more intelligent, more informed,
more congruent with responsibly held, defensible beliefs.

Chapter Four: "Practice Theory" and Praxis

"Practice Theory" and Praxialism

The idea of music as social praxis challenges speculative-rationalist aesthetic theories of music and musical value. Praxial thinking acknowledges that music has many easily recognized, affective (aisthesic) attractions that are well suited to its many social roles and to the endless list of personal and social functions that give rise to the existence of different musics to begin with. The praxialism urged herein advances a clearly pragmatic and empirical alternative to aesthetic speculations.

Appreciation as Use; Music Teaching as Promoting Use

Instead of premising 'music appreciation' as a mystical aesthetic matter, praxis takes *empirical* notice of the ways in which people actually *use*—incorporate— music in their everyday lives. It does not depend, therefore, on teaching "background knowledge" as a prior condition of appreciation. Instead, it emphasizes that knowledge for promoting musical dispositions and choices comes from dedicated, loving *use*. Such *praxial knowledge* is therefore grounded in 'real-life' evidence of music's social relevance.

Making a Pragmatic Difference

Pragmatism in philosophy does not refer to easily expedient actions. Instead, 'truth' is the actual difference a proposition or claim makes in contending with the practical challenges and conditions of 'real life.' Thus, the pragmatic criterion of a praxially oriented music education asks: What can students *do* musically, at all (i.e., newly), better, with more benefits and rewards, and with a more positive disposition for regular use in life?

Chapter Five: Praxis as an Alternative to Aesthetic Theory

Theoria for Contemplation

Aristotle's three-part account of knowledge proposes the concept of *theoria*. Today that would include higher mathematics, analytic philosophy, and science. But the active form of theoria is *contemplation* for its own sake. It was therefore undertaken only by scholars. Theory that served praxis was demoted to the status of craft-skill and 'applied' knowledge.

Techne and Artisanal Making

Aristotle's second category of knowledge was *techne*: skill, craft-competence, and technical knowledge. Aspects of this category involve matters of musical performance techniques. But, for Aristotle, "excellent making" involved creating 'things' that served their uncontroversial purposes well. Any relation to performance techniques, pursued as though for their own sake, is remote for Aristotle. For him, 'good' flute playing served worthy praxial conditions.

Praxis and Prudence in Aristotle

Techne is concerned with 'things,' while *praxis* serves the needs of people. It therefore has an *ethical* dimension. This ethical "prudence" (*phronesis*) requires that agents be '*care*-full' to bring about promised benefits (*eupraxia*). Only tangibly beneficial results for those served qualify as praxis: Anything less amounts to *dyspraxia* or, in the case of doing harm to people, professional mal-praxis (i.e., malpractice).

Praxis in Contemporary Society and Culture

In the cultural and social sciences, praxis involves the various institutions and ideologies that have been influenced by the past at the same time that they shape a 'way of life' and its associated values. The sociability that fuels music's role in society and culture involves the various social functions that are added to (or that organize) sound in serving different social purposes and functions, everything from a lullaby to a brass fanfare.

Chapter Six: Praxis in Music and Music Education

Praxis as a Noun

As a *noun*, praxis entails a notable (and ethical) *result*. Music in this sense is a product or end result created to serve certain social or personal circumstances, conditions, and needs—needs that are the reasons that bring a particular musical praxis into existence to begin with. Music education as praxis is thus focused on tangible and pragmatic results for students and on the contributions made in the long run to their musical lives and to society.

Praxis as Action

Praxis as a *verb* form refers to act*ing*. In music, it is a do*ing* or a try*ing* to of a musical kind (or at least to which music is central). The difference is exemplified by "love" as a collective noun (e.g., "I am 'in' love") versus "loving" as a quality of acting. Furthermore, such doing (e.g., loving music) is its own reward.

Praxial Knowledge

Praxis also generates practical (praxial) knowledge: the pragmatic 'know how,' 'how to,' or 'can do' that arises from the verb form of praxis—from 'doing' music. It thus arises from experience with praxis as a noun: learning from effective results for the musical praxis at stake. Importantly, praxial knowledge develops *from* praxis, not as a *precondition* of praxis: learning by doing, not before doing.

Chapter Seven: Action Learning and "Breaking 100 in Music"

Action Learning

Action learning is a *curriculum model* rooted in praxialism and pragmatism. Thus, it is focused on putting into action (praxis) models of musical sociality in society that are inviting to students and that, therefore, have a likelihood of developing dispositions and attitudes that favor an active life of making and enjoying music throughout life.

"Breaking 100 in Music"

This motto implies a criterion for the praxial approach to music described here. In bowling, breaking 100 (i.e., scoring above 100) is the goal; in golf, breaking 100 (i.e., scoring below) motivates participation and practice. Music lacks numerical scores. But helping students to "break 100" is a psychological "tipping point" that (as in sports) motivates a lifelong love of an amateur activity that is life enhancing.

Music Teaching as and for Praxis

When music is understood as a valuable social praxis, music education should be understood as social praxis that advances the praxis of music and its social rewards. A praxial view of teaching praxis attaches an ethical criterion of success in terms of the *value added by music education* to what students enter school with. Successful teaching, then, is qualified not just in musical terms but also in social and ethical terms.

PREFACE

This monograph offers a short introduction to music and music education philosophy as *social praxis*. (The habit of many authors in stressing the "social" in that description is retained, even though praxis is usually social.) This introduction to a *contemporary* philosophy of music education is based on a variety of scholarly sources. Many are from social science disciplines that are usually absent in the education of musicians and music educators but are nonetheless useful to understanding the nature and value of music (i.e., what 'it' *is*). This clarification can benefit those who teach it. However, to be clear: This is a philosophical study supported by findings of various social disciplines, not a sociological study.

I try not to wade into scholarly discourse in great detail or with forbidding academic language. The related readings at the end of each chapter allow readers to learn more about any particular issue that interests them. Even readers not interested in the scholarship that supports the philosophy offered can, by perusing the references, understand that considerable research exists on behalf of a praxial philosophy of music and music education. The use of scientific evidence for philosophy is relatively new and still quite rare, so the amassed evidence should not be ignored or discounted.

Annotations are provided where the title does not clearly indicate the relevance to a chapter or the concerns at stake in this study. These annotations, even for those who do not follow up on a topic, nonetheless give some sense of the support for the praxial philosophy offered. They are, however, only a shorthand account to guide readers interested in further examination of the evidence. But, for scholars, the related readings offer a realm of scholarship not typically considered in mainstream music education discourse. Those sources also offer a fund of further studies (in their own citations) that address the divide between orthodox *aesthetic* accounts of music and *social* accounts. Filling that gap, as regards all levels of music education, is one of the reasons for this study.

The readings given in support particularly of Part One should, first of all, put off any facile accusation of the "straw man" fallacy in philosophy whereby a position is articulated in terms that unfairly subject it to easy critique. More than ample support for the critique is offered, based on both philosophical and various social science disciplines. Second, critical reviews that do not take this range of scholarship into thoughtful consideration (i.e., actually consult it) cannot be taken seriously, since the supporting references from the social sciences in support of praxial thinking (that are most usually ignored when they differ with aesthetic theories) are—as I hope the study will make clear—at variance with the host of too easily accepted institutional ideologies that are usually fiercely defended by status quo advocates.

Along critical lines, I should respond (with thanks) to a reply of one student in the trial of this book who wrote that, despite agreeing with its premises, she or he still "liked" 'classical' music. The present study is in not at all a complaint against such music. It is, instead, an attempt to advance the idea that "music," and its many powers and benefits, extends far beyond the audience listening praxis for 'classical' music. My position is that "music" and "music education" as praxis are much more important than only a traditional concern with the 'classics': that both music and music education should properly embrace *all* musics and their important contributions to society, culture, and the life well lived. The general argument is that the aesthetic ideology sells short the many roles and benefits of music in and for life.

Even though attempting to be as brief as possible in introducing music and music education as social praxis, I have tried to avoid superficially skimming over important matters that deserve some detail. Thus, each chapter explores topics and concerns (marked †) that are the foundation for follow-up, detailed, and elaborated discussions and conclusions in later chapters (their reappearance in new contexts is also marked with the same symbol to alert readers to the connection of later to earlier discussions). This overlap is, thus, not a matter of simple repetition but a planned writing model that expands on earlier ideas according to later, new topics and considerations in the manner of what is called a *spiral curriculum*. In subsequent sections and chapters, then, issues discussed in earlier chapters are intentionally revisited and expanded with amplified relevance to the new topical focus of each chapter.

This has an advantage for typical readers who aren't likely to read the text from beginning to end in one sitting (or who are assigned only selected chapters—which I hope won't happen often) and who thus can profit from encountering again in amplified contexts in later chapters ideas that have been discussed earlier from different perspectives. Thus, readers who notice the return of previous ideas should attend to the implications of their *new* context.

I hope to have achieved some sort of balance between the detailed interests of scholars and those more general concerns of pre- and in-service teachers. The scholars want more detail, teachers are satisfied with less. In consideration of this delicate balance, scholars should consult the supporting readings. They offer a realm of research seldom covered in music education scholarship. I hope that teachers (and teachers-to-be), on the other hand, will be interested enough to sample some of the interesting and vital evidence that supports the contentions of this study. The praxial philosophy advanced herein may well be controversial because of its departure from aesthetic rationales of music, but the amassed evidence from the various social sciences, otherwise excluded from the education of music teachers, needs to be consulted and weighed before one can dismiss it.

The ideas included here, then, stem from current and classical scholarly sources from a variety of disciplines. They are important if teaching is to be informed by more than recipe-like 'delivery methods'—that is, by methods that are focused on 'delivering' instruction (lessons, rehearsals) but not on what or whether any knowledge or skill is actually learned that is long lasting and musically life enriching. I seek to convey these scholarly ideas in straight-forward and not too technical terms (except where unavoidable) suited to a wide range of readers and interests.

To this end, I also avoid scholarly citations in favor of the end-of-chapter related readings that are keyed by * in the text. Trial use of earlier stages of this manuscript showed that pre- and in-service teachers approved of this approach and of the economical and clear style of writing that they do not have to strug-gle to understand. The occasional parenthetical insertions are, I hope, less of a distraction to readers than endnotes and citations would be. Maybe some are even entertaining or enlightening.

Goals

My intent is to provide a clear basis by which a praxial philosophy of music and music education can be applied in a variety of foundation and methods courses (called *didactics*, in Europe) and contexts in music education. Thus, I do not deal with the many important "how to" practical details offered in such courses. Instead, a praxial philosophy of Action Learning is offered about 'why' to teach music in schools and 'what' of music that could be taught is most worthwhile to teach (i.e., curriculum).† Some examples of didactic "how to" (or "not to") suggestions are offered where they illustrate what otherwise would be an abstract idea. But my intent is for such pedagogical details to be addressed by the professor's class activities, assignments, and other readings based on the specialized focus of each course—thus, differently in, say, a con-ducting course than in a general music methods course.

The intention of this study, then, is to help provide a warranted *philosophi-cal foundation* (i.e., as based on scholarly evidence from the social sciences) for a variety of specialized courses—foundations of and introductions to music education courses, general music and instrumental methods, music education conducting courses, and the like. Its short chapters facilitate use as comple-mentary assigned reading, for discussion, assignments, and other applications according to the course focus.

Readership

The reading is intended to be suitable for various levels of music education, including upper undergraduate levels, where students are often left unchallenged by and uniformed of such foundational ideas (e.g., curriculum theory). The use of earlier versions of the manuscript with junior-level music education majors (at the SUNY Fredonia School of Music) has helpfully confirmed that not only are they able to understand such ideas; they are also inclined and receptive to philosophical discourse. They have given me the impression that not only are they interested in such discourse, but they relish having status quo assumptions challenged. The ideas offered here are also intended to be a corrective to current practices and traditions in music teaching. They seek to help teachers move away from status quo teaching that has put music education under mounting threat to its very existence. Such teaching too often falls short of its claims to be "basic" in notable enough ways that convince taxpayers and education authorities that it contributes to an enriched personhood and to a good life lived in part through music.†

The approach here is *carefully* mindful that in the arts, a critique (for example, offered by an effective music lesson) is intended to be both *corrective* and *constructive*. Imagine if the response of a teacher at a music lesson was always "That was great!" Music teachers in particular should thus recognize this two-step pedagogical model without taking offense about their teaching. Just as was effective in attaining and refining their musical skills, teaching needs the kind of critique and coaching that produce progress and improvement.

However, for most teachers, once the student teaching internship is over and they face the 'real world' of teaching year after year, little in the way of critical input is available (certainly not from the usual reviews by those principals who know little about music education). Thus, what follows is intended to contribute to the kind of self-reflection on the part of music teachers that can lead to what has been called "reflective practice": the habit of those in the helping professions (e.g., medicine, therapy, ministry) to honestly reflect on the premises and results of their praxis. As a result, I hope the text can be especially useful for in-service teachers.

Using this Book

I seek to endorse a down-to-earth *praxial alternative* to the often taken-for-granted assumption held by many music teachers that music education is only a *subcategory* of aesthetic education and that, therefore, any music activity or experience provided in school is automatically aesthetic and thus educationally valuable. This easily made claim, of course, cannot be assessed or demonstrated since responding to music is a personal, inward experience, not outwardly observable. This fact has led to the mounting need for advocacy on behalf of school music; the public clearly has not been impressed with unverifiable aesthetic claims for music education. Instead, the scholarship offered here advances music education as *music* education.

Music teachers know a lot about music but typically very little about aesthetics. Yet many have often unwittingly relied on noble-sounding aesthetic assumptions as a rationale for their teaching ethos. Those taken-for-granted claims will be critically examined in Part One in order to demonstrate their speculative nature and pragmatic unsuitability as either a rationale for or a systematic philosophy of music education. Part Two offers a proposed praxial and evidence-based alternative. In sum, then, I seek to promote a relevant and useful (useable) understanding of an Action Learning curricular model of praxialism for music teachers.

Different scholars have offered perspectives on a variety of praxial themes (amply referenced at the ends of chapters). Yet their agreement and overlapping on the *action (generative) ideal* of praxis (one that 'generates' dialogue around a shared theme) are frequent and mutually reinforcing. They all begin with the proposal that "music" is an important social practice, not a museum of 'works' visited on rare leisure-time occasions of concert and recital attendance, although those are certainly one important social role of music. Given the mounting diversity of scholarship on music and music education as praxial, it would be presumptuous to offer the model proposed here as "the" (as in "only") praxial stance.

Again, considerable attention is given throughout to the critique of the aesthetic ideology and in support for praxialism of relevant scholarly substantiation from social theory, sociology, cultural studies, cultural history, cultural anthropology, and the many other disciplines that are typically *excluded* in the preparation of future musicians and music teachers. Thus, far too often, music teachers don't know enough about this range of research to apply it to their teaching praxis. My hope is that readers will find this scholarship interesting, relevant, and, most of all, useful.

ACKNOWLEDGMENTS

I have learned much from the many teachers who have followed a praxial persuasion and whose teaching success has demonstrated that music education can lead to lifelong musical abilities and dispositions. In particular, I am indebted to the winner of the first (2014) *Grammy Teaching Award in Music*, Kent Knappenberger (see citations in Chapters 6 and 7). His program in a small school in western New York has produced many notable and attention-earning praxial results and has been a direct inspiration for more than a few of the perspectives described in this monograph and is a valuable confirmation of the praxial premise. My thanks also go to Laura Dornberger (SUNY Fredonia), whose use of earlier stages of the manuscript provided very useful comments from several classes of junior music education majors in a Foundations of Music Education course. Feedback from Laura and her students over the course of a month of lessons based on this study gives me confidence that the writing and ideas are intelligible and interesting and promote the intended critically reflective perspective on music education philosophy. I am also indebted to Wayne Bowman and David J. Elliott for their constant philosophical inspiration, feedback, and professional friendship, especially about praxis. Finally, the last stages of this study profited from suggestions offered by Hildegard Froehlich, Marie McCarthy, and (again) Laura Dornberger. Many of their comments and recommendations have improved the book, but, given the need to "write short," I take responsibility for any advice that could not be followed.

Part One

IDEOLOGY CRITIQUE

INTRODUCTION

> Although philosophy does have its own unique areas of enquiry,
> one of its most distinctive features is not so much **what** you study
> as **how** you study it—and it is this what makes the experience of
> studying philosophy quite different from that of any other subject.
> In philosophy, we learn to identify, and think carefully about, our
> most basic ideas and theories—those that support all the questing
> for knowledge we do in other subject areas. . . . We look behind our
> everyday concerns to examine the systems and structures which
> support our thinking (and which ordinarily we take for granted),
> and to test their soundness.
>
> C. Saunders, D. Mossley, G. MacDonald Ross,
> and D. Lamb*

Some readers may have concluded that a philosophy of music education (or a philosophy of anything) is an academic, intellectual endeavor doomed to misadventure, wasting time, and frustration. Furthermore, they may believe that philosophy is the domain of philosophers whose preoccupations have little to do with 'real life' and—as with the debates between medieval scholastic philosophers about how many angels can fit on the head of a pin—that its concerns are "merely academic." Yet this view of philosophy and its relevance to life and teaching music is misleadingly mistaken.*

First of all, people hold many philosophies that are *tacit*. These philosophical beliefs are expressed not in words but through people's actions and thus are often taken for granted. Nonetheless, such tacit philosophies* govern people's many actions, often without any rational support that can be defended according to philosophical criteria. Take for example the tacit beliefs behind racism. Often, the holders of such philosophical beliefs (e.g., racists) resent when the actions promoted by their tacit philosophies are called into question (as Part One of this study may do for some readers already under the tacit influence of the aesthetic ideology).

Hence, "philosophy" is often held at two levels: what has been called philosophy with a small "p" and philosophy with a capital "P." Small "p" philosophy

3

is given to various pronouncements and stances—tacit or not—that are not usually recognized by the holder *as* philosophy, but they *are* beliefs held in a weak sense of small "p" philosophy. For example, such beliefs as "my philosophy is spare the rod and spoil the child," or that "evolution should be taught only as a theory" (many "shoulds" are small "p"), or that "the place of a woman should be in the home," or that "government is the problem, not the solution to the problem"—these examples all qualify as small "p" philosophy for lacking substance (evidence) and cogent and consistent arguments. Most people have a host of such small "p" convictions that guide their actions and values. They just don't realize that they do, so they take their philosophical beliefs to be logically sound and beyond dispute—until they are questioned. Then they often reply defensively (and sometimes angrily). These are often not rationale moments and are best avoided. ("Try to reason with a fool and you are called foolish," the saying goes.)

Arguments about "love," for example, often break down on differences of small "p," tacit philosophies. For such philosophies, "love" is a psychological state of mind into which you "fall" (as though into an uncovered manhole), after which you deal (or not) with the conditions into which you have "fallen." Or, too often, when those conditions prove to be no longer agreeable or productive—and depending on how 'deep' the 'manhole' is into which you have "fallen"—you have considerable difficulty getting out of the 'hole' in to which you have fallen, Or, you wonder about whether coping is worth it, as opposed to getting out and seeking to "fall" again, more successfully elsewhere.

This Western philosophy of "romantic love" is totally in contrast to the traditional Eastern philosophy, which prescribes arranged marriages based on social compatibility and other criteria. As a result, the couple, over time—that is, *after* marriage—develop a working and "loving" relationship (although "love marriages" based on Western models are becoming more common in the East). In either the Western or Eastern sense, however, philosophically, "love" is best seen in a "loving" (shared, positive social) relationship over time, not as an emotional or cognitive state of mutual attraction (especially physical) that precedes and leads to marriage. (Later the "love of music" described in terms of 'music appreciation' will be considered.)† Clearly, divorce rates prove the small "p" philosophy of "romantic love" to be problematic. Obviously, a lot of people "fall out of" love on this philosophical premise.* (And many students 'fall' out of love with music—or, more precisely, with *school music*—and quit lessons or ensembles and mentally 'drop out' in classes.)

Capital "P" philosophies seek, instead, to reach reasoned conclusions as to what is "true, good, and beautiful" (as the cliché) goes. They are philosophies that attempt to *warrant*, through systematic 'argument' with those of other philosophical persuasions, rationales, and traditional conclusions, ideas that might benefit those who are thus convinced. Or, following Emmanuel Kant (i.e., his 'critical' platform for philosophy), they systematically challenge and thus clarify philosophies whose 'arguments' are deficient or of the small "p" variety. (The current monograph is an attempt in the spirit of this critical platform to challenge various aesthetic theories that rely mistakenly on Kant's theory of "free beauty" as a theory of art.)†

There are, of course, capital "P" philosophies whose arguments are obscure and of interest mainly to other philosophers. But the most powerful of these, over time, usually elicit the kind and degree of dialogue that brings about commentary and response from others that progressively clarify basic philosophical issues of philosophical consequence and importance to life. Philosophical newcomers don't at first know or care about such issues. But, in what follows here, the hope is that the many issues surrounding the philosophy of music and music education *do* make an important difference to what, how, and why music is taught in schools.

Music teachers, of course, have all kinds of beliefs about music, students, and education that are rooted in small "p" philosophies about human nature, children's development, learning, and what "music" *is*—too often held in the face of scholarship and capital "P" philosophies to the contrary. For example, they may believe that a child's mind is a "blank slate" (*tabula rasa*) waiting to be 'written on' by education; that music is a collection of 'works'; that punishment is an effective teaching approach to student motivation for learning and good behavior; that competition sorts the 'wheat from the chaff' and that the musically *select few* thus rise to the top; that the learning process is the same for students regardless of their stage of development and level of schooling; that childhood is basically an 'animalistic' stage on the way to adulthood and that children thus need to be 'trained' in civilized ways; or that learning is a matter of individual attainment (Piaget), not a result of social conditions in life or in the classroom (Vygotsky). And typical small "p" philosophies of music assume, as is too often said, that "music is the language of emotions" (ignoring the differences between 'real' emotions and 'aesthetic emotions' that the philosophy of music is concerned with) or that "music is organized sound" (without questioning why or how it is organized and the meaning of different sounds and different organizations of sounds).†

In music education, then, several small "p" philosophical themes are forever current. One involves beliefs about musical 'talent': the (small "p") philosophy that some students 'have it' and others just don't. Thus, correspondingly, efforts on behalf of those who don't 'have it' are wasted because "you can't get blood from a stone." Another is the philosophy behind "no pain, no gain" pedagogies—the philosophical assumption that music is a "discipline" and therefore requires rigor and sacrifice (and woe be unto those who don't submit). Those who fall by the wayside (i.e., quit ensembles or music lessons) are thus seen by holders of this philosophy as thereby allowing a teacher to devote the time saved from efforts in behalf of the 'untalented' many to the 'talented' few. This just encourages an *elitism* that contradicts the usual agenda of school music's ideology as contributing to the general education of *all* students—an elitism that is properly opposed by social critics in and outside music education.†

This elitist philosophy takes for granted the premise that school music *properly* functions as a kind pre-conservatory training, despite the fact that even the most able and motivated students most often do not want to make a career of music. What percentage of graduating students seeks musical careers? And, of those few, how many succeed? And how were the musical lives of rest of the graduates benefited musically by their years in school music ensembles?

Consider, for example, that premises about 'talent' can be compared to the doctor who complains that all the patients in the waiting room are sick! However, in the *helping professions* (e.g., medicine, therapy, clergy, law, nursing, teaching), the governing action ideal† of "help" implies conditions and symptoms that need assistance and support. Correspondingly, a helping profession is ethically engaged in problem-solving that is focused on the difficulties facing people (e.g., patients, students), not on the preferences, pleasures, and profits of the practitioner.

Other small "p" philosophical beliefs center on inherited notions about what "education" is and what schooling (the verb form) is 'good for'. Given the diverse historical and philosophical roots of the word "education," should it be a philosophy based on (a) *ēducāre*, putting knowledge into otherwise passive and empty minds? Or should it be on (b) *ēdūcere*, 'drawing out' (educing) and developing knowledge from a naturally receptive mind? The first philosophy (a) leads to lecture teaching, enforced skill-drill, memorization, filling minds with information, and paper-and-pencil testing (and usually student boredom and resistance). The second philosophy (b) leads to learning by doing, active involvement, and acknowledging and following the natural interests of learners. In the case of music, this second philosophy means building school music curricula† on the many attractions that students have to music—beginning in early childhood before school—and 'drawing out' whatever musical capacities they are capable of or interested in developing.

The choice should be clear for music teachers. These are not inconsequential philosophical differences. Only a moment's recollection probably brings to the reader's mind the memory of teachers—in music or other subjects—who were examples of each—and their problems and benefits.

Music education philosophy therefore shares in the tensions arising from this contradiction between philosophies. The question at stake, then, is whether (a) music education should be a matter of 'programming' the brain to be aesthetically receptive to music and 'converting' students from 'popular' musics to 'good' music. Or (b) is it instead a matter of encouraging and developing a latent and natural musical potential in all people for musicking?

With the former philosophy (a), music will be 'imposed' on the blank minds (*tabula rasa*) of students in order to 'cultivate' their aesthetic responsiveness, as premised by aesthetic philosophy. In the praxial philosophy (b), instead, *all* students will be seen as innately imbued with some capacity for music that can enhance their lives. Importantly, then, an assumption of philosophy (a), that students who have no musical 'talent' can be shunted aside and ignored in school music, is decisively *rejected* by supporters of (b) and praxialists. In support of (b), cultural anthropology instead privileges the view that humans have a natural capacity for and inclination "to music" (as the *verb form*: what, hereafter, will be called *musicking* (also spelled *musicing*)—'doing' music in some form).† In this scientific view, humans are as naturally inclined to music and art (consider early cave painting, for example) as they are to language.*

What follows in this study is a philosophy of music and music education *social praxis* based on the evidence from the social sciences: that music and art are a *natural* part of the endowment of human nature and, thus, are *natural* expressions of being human. Furthermore, it is premised on the view, again from the scientific researches of anthropology and sociology, that humans are *naturally* social beings: that a major trait of human nature is a strong inborn disposition for engaging in various forms of *sociality*. And, the social sciences (especially cultural studies) are agreed on the view that culture and society involve and are the results of social praxis (of all kinds). Moreover, among the most important examples of social praxis are art and music. Together, they help create society and account for some its fullest and finest flowering.*

However, the prevailing philosophy of music education in the past half-century (not to be confused with the philosophy of *music*) has been based on the philosophical premise of *ēducāre*: that music is *not* a 'natural' human interest, ability, or trait. In consequence, the *cultural* expression of music needs to be 'disciplined' into people (especially students) in order for music's 'cultural heritage' to be properly fulfilled and perpetuated. In particular, then, the *aesthetic theory of art** uncritically assumes the philosophical thesis that "culture" (and civilization) is a human development that arises (in some generic form) in history and thereafter needs concentrated discipline, study, and 'cultivation' to be maintained. The difference, then, is over whether culture creates music and art or whether music and art are natural human expressions that (like language) create culture and society to begin with. Argued here, with support from the sociology of music, ethnomusicology, cultural studies, and cultural anthropology, is a capital "P" philosophy based on praxis that supports the second alternative.

In the spirit of "critical philosophy," then (e.g., as indicated in the Chapter Overview epigram for this book), the "confused" and confusing aesthetic philosophy of art and music needs to be subjected to critical appraisal as a basis for a defensible (capital "P") philosophy of music education (Part One). Unlike most analytic philosophy that relies exclusively on reason, the capital "P' philosophy offered here relies heavily on empirical evidence from the many social sciences that are disregarded in the education of most musicians and teachers.

Then, in Part Two, an alternate and more philosophically and scientifically "defensible" (see the epigram again) capital "P" philosophy of music education is proposed on the basis of the plentiful and all too obvious *evidence* from the social sciences that music is a major social praxis in contemporary and social history. Thus, in what follows, music and art are seen as being as natural to 'humans being human' as language is and the proper role of music education is seen as a philosophy based on *ēdūcere*: the 'drawing out' and developing of musical capacities that are a natural birthright of *all* students, not of just the supposedly talented few.

As shall be shown, aesthetic ideology is a very false and misleading account of why music is so important to human society. Musical "culture," in history and in the modern world, is not the icing on the cake of civilization. It is part of the *whole* cake, icing and all (even licking the plate).

. . .

Aesthetic Theory and the Spectatorship/ Connoisseurship Theory of 'Fine Art'

To begin with, then, an effective philosophy of the role of *music education in general education* (i.e., for all students) requires a clear and warranted philosophical understanding of what "music" *is* and is 'good for'.[1] Until quite recently, Western theories of music and musical value have been based largely in the theoretical assumptions and terms of what has been called the *aesthetic theory of art*† that took shape in the mid-eighteenth century.† This theory has in fact since multiplied into a confusing array of competing and conflicting aesthetic theories. Although they share a certain overlapping of similar terms and topics (discussed throughout Part One), the differences between different aesthetic theories of art are, at heart, irreconcilable. Aestheticians just don't agree with each other very much! Moreover, the aesthetic theory of art is only one *philosophy of art*, but it has had and continues to have a considerable impact on music education. Part One explains some of the key reasons why that theory is disputed (even by philosophers of art, but especially by analytic philosophers), and why it provides a very weak foundation for music education in schools.

The theories that generally advance the aesthetic theory of art generally share what I call the *speculative-rationalist* mindset: "speculative" because they amount to conjecture, and "rationalist" because they rely on abstract reason rather than empirical evidence concerning how people actually respond to art and music and why every society values art and music. *Nothing you will read in the literature of aesthetics will enhance your appreciation of music.*

---

1 Words, concepts, and familiar phrases indicated with single quotation marks either involve a special and restricted use of the word in question (e.g., references to 'good for') or serve as shorthand for "supposed" or "so-called" (e.g., 'good music', 'real-life', 'talent'). Also, the term "praxis" is sometimes used in distinction to "practice" (as shall be qualified in later chapters). Care should be taken, however, *not* to equate "praxis" with "practice" when the latter is understood as manifesting routines and habits that *do not* meet the ethical and social criteria of praxis explained in later chapters.

Nothing! This is more than evident in the many published "companions" and "compendiums" of aesthetics that are intended to guide readers through the endless jungle of aesthetic theorizing, its terms and many enigmas.* Even a casual reader can note fundamental conflicts between authors within a particular guide and between endlessly proliferating publications on the topic. (Are so many needed because aesthetic theory is so convoluted and contested?)

Despite their endless disagreements, the collective effect of these speculative-rationalist theories has typically advanced *spectatorship theories* of art and music as 'fine' (or 'high' art).* Hence, the 'fine arts' are said to exist simply in order to be *contemplated* in rare moments of leisure (thus the "spectatorship" designation, meaning watching or listening for its own sake and not otherwise being engaged), according to what has since been called an *aesthetic attitude*.† This mindset is said to promote "pure" aesthetic experience, "free" of values that are influenced by personal and subjective needs. Thus, in music, listeners are supposed to focus solely on "aesthetic properties" (or "qualities") that are listened to "for their own sake" and not for what many aestheticians call "extra-musical" *functions* (such as music's use in religion and celebration).†

Music that is 'good for' such typical social and everyday pragmatic uses has been correspondingly devalued for not being "disinterested," for being "dependent" on 'real-life' connections.† In other words, it is *de*valued for being useful and down to earth in its sociopersonal meanings and, therefore, for being insufficiently cerebral and distanced from everyday life. In general, then, speculative-rationalist aesthetic theories of music have denied the fully *embodied* nature—the important role of the body†—in musical responding. Accordingly, *bodily* experiences (e.g., visceral chills or thrills, physical reactions of music) are viewed as unbecoming in comparison to *cerebralized* 'aesthetic appreciation'.*

As a result, certain ever-popular compositions have been elevated to the status of Great Works: veritable monuments of Western civilization. This standard repertory of Western classical music (and, for some, jazz, with its own repertory) has occupied the attention of aesthetes, cognoscenti, and those who aspire to 'classy' or elite taste and the social status of 'high' culture.

An *aesthetic hierarchy*† has thus in effect been created and tacitly acknowledged in the minds of connoisseurs that has "pure" instrumental music (i.e., music without words or programmatic inferences—namely chamber music, such as string quartets, solo instruments, and symphonies) at the very top as the highest, most esoteric, and learned forms of musical culture. Opera, choral music, and art song are found somewhere in the middle of this hierarchy because of the "extra-musical" meanings conveyed by the worldly references of words.* All vernacular, 'popular', and everyday musics (e.g., religious musics, folk, ethnic, patriotic, and dance music) have therefore been relegated to the lower regions of the hierarchy—if allowed on the aesthetic hierarchy at all by cultural patrons, aesthetes, and other mindguards of musical virtue.

One unfortunate negative effect is that this hierarchy also tends to mirror musically or even create key socioeconomic *class differences.*† The more "highbrow" a type of music is on the aesthetic hierarchy (e.g., chamber music, symphonies), the more likely it is to appeal to the more 'cultivated', educated, upper socioeconomic levels of society. Accordingly, the more vernacular or 'popular' and easily accessible the music is to 'uncultivated' audiences, the more "lowbrow" it is on the implied aesthetic hierarchy. Therefore, the more widespread such "lowbrow" music is with lower-middle-class and blue-collar workers—who in turn steadfastly avoid "highbrow" music.* However, sometimes "lowbrow" music is also popular with the more educated, upper socioeconomic class, whose musical tastes have been found by music sociologists to be more omnivorous and thus wide-ranging.*

Unfortunately, given the high costs of 'high' culture (and the two *are* related!), outside university communities, most people cannot afford to attend concerts, operas, and recitals (even in countries where these are subsidized by government). Thus, they most often choose a steady diet of musics that are immediately appealing and easily accessible. They are also less likely to be interested in school music or music lessons for their children (lessons and instruments cost money). And their penny-pinching extends to their reluctance to pay taxes that support school music programs (though in the United States they usually rally their economic support for sports programs—which tells us something about their values).

Praxis and "Practice Theory"

In 1991, the aesthetician Philip Alperson, at the time the editor of *The Journal of Aesthetics and Art Criticism*, published a paper arguing that a philosophy of music, and thus of music education, should properly account for *all* forms and kinds of musical *praxis*, not just music at the top of the orthodox aesthetic hierarchy.* The idea of praxis in philosophy (i.e., Aristotle)† and classical sociological theory† (which Alperson ignored) has resulted in a growing literature concerning *praxial* approaches to music education.† This new philosophical scholarship has had a mounting impact on music education philosophy, curriculum, and methods (didactics) around the world, perhaps especially in North America.*

Praxial thinking in music and music education also gains support from the rise of the "practice turn"† in contemporary social philosophy, sociology, and cultural studies.* (Again, the reader is reminded that the terms "praxis" and "practice" can sometimes be used interchangeably. However, as is explained in Part Two, there is a type of 'doing' that is often attached in certain contexts to the term "praxis" and that distinguishes it from a "practice" as a traditional "custom" or "habit"—in particular, the relevant ethical and social ideals that praxis entails.)† The scholars of this "practice turn" study how individuals, societies, and cultures are created and sustained by and through the collective spirit and praxis of the social institutions and institutional ideologies in which they are involved.*

The resulting "practice theory"† offers a corrective balance—indeed, a major challenge—to accounts of social order based simply on interpretations that credit "society" as being the result of the collective agreement of individuals. A natural human impulse to *sociality*—not individuality!—and the interlocked network of human praxis it generates and sustains (and that, in turn, over time shapes sociality and society) best explain our psycho-social sense of "Being" (i.e., our individual and collective identity). Paradoxically, society makes possible individuality, if by no other criterion than by standing out from others.

Importantly, then, practice theory accounts for (a) the strong social influences on our individual cognition, consciousness, and states of mind; (b) the social sources of our knowledge, values, and even emotions; (c) how a society, culture, or subculture is organized, reproduced, transmitted, and transformed; and (d) the social institutions that we populate and that live in and through us.* In practice theory, institutional social membership is, as one author puts it, "the site of the social,"* a source for promoting all kinds of sociality. Thus, it is a primary source of the "social mind" taken note of by social philosophy and pragmatism.* As evidence of the sociality of music, consider whether you listen to Zen *shaku hachi* flute music, or polkas, or Māori shell trumpets. If you do, you know that each has a different social function or use in its own cultural situation and tradition.

Indeed, for practice theory, being an individual with a specific identity is the result of participation and learning in a complex network of social practices and interactions. We are individuals, then, both by contrast with and in terms of our participation in an interlocking web of such sociocultural endeavors. The "I" at any moment is differently influenced according to the timing and location of our immediate praxial contexts—everything in the place or space of a social praxis—in which we act with particular purposes and *roles* (e.g., "life as theater"—sociological Dramaturgy) where we 'play' (act out) the generally scripted roles of our social world. For example, "I" can 'be' a teacher in the school context, a wife to my husband, a soccer mom to my children, a daughter, daughter-in-law, Catholic, food pantry helper, and so on, according to the particular roles expected in each social context.

The *expressive body* itself, too, is a socially mediated result of the mind, and the mind itself is an expression of the socially influenced body (e.g., the 'ample' bodies of women in Rubens's paintings compared to today's fashion models).† Our body and how we interact with others are socially determined: for example, the differences in cultural norms regulating how near to stand in a conversation or how clothing traditions are related to social praxis concerning the publicly presented body (i.e., beyond weather). But also consider different religious traditions governing the body, especially as regards women's dress in some societies.

In this, practice theory rejects the mind-body separation of pre-Renaissance†
philosophies where the role of the body is denied or depreciated.† This role
of the *expressive* body is, of course, especially central to praxial accounts of
music since the body is centrally engaged in and by music. Indeed, the bodily
gestures of performers that we can't help noticing often become part of "the
music" as we hear it. This is one advantage of listening to live performances
rather than recordings. This gestural element is typically ignored by aesthetes,
other than to be critiqued if it detracts from "the music" as "pure" sound forms.
(Recordings therefore eliminate this aspect of "the music."† This can be an
important loss.)

So the body is largely ignored or minimized by speculative-rationalist aesthetics that instead favor the "pure," rational, and cerebral contemplation of
music. In consequence, bodily responses are denigrated as aesthetically inferior forms of merely hedonistic aural stimulation (e.g., 'heavy metal') or as
poor audience etiquette (e.g., any physical movements that reflect a musical
response, such as to a syncopation). As audience members, then, we have been
taught, socially, to not 'conduct' along with the symphony or otherwise move
or bodily reveal our musical responses. We are thus trained by the community
of aesthetes and cultural patrons in history who have developed an audience
etiquette that reflects their purely cerebral regard for music in almost total
denial of the bodily bases of musical responding.*

In music education discourse, the term *praxialism* includes strong influences
from leading practice theorists and from the long history of the concept of
praxis that existed long before the concept of 'classical' or 'art' music was
created and long before the concepts of aesthetics and the idea of the 'fine
arts' were invented. The idea of music as a praxis, for everyday or for special
(usually communal) uses, first appeared in ancient Greece† and gets modified,
extended, even transformed in a variety of contemporary uses, including current pragmatic and social philosophy.†

While reference to praxialism today may seem to suggest a convergence of
ideas, there are some variants between praxialists in music and music education.* However, as qualified in the Preface, the basic and shared premise of
these theories is that what we call "music" is a thoroughly social praxis. It
is not a repository or canon (or museum collection) of traditionally favored
'works' that exists to be 'appreciated' aesthetically via "pure" (and supposedly
purifying) contemplation alone.

In fact, the many different social functions to which music is central account
for how and why different musics come into being in the first place. Each kind of
music is thus attuned from its very beginning to the ways in which it is intended
to be used and enjoyed and for which it is produced and performed: music *for*
concert listening, dancing, religious music, patriotic music, celebratory music,
and so on. Any praxis—each type of musical engagement—involves countless
social elements that are responsible for the distinctive differences among various
musics (e.g., lullabies, jazz, patriotic music, popular 'love' songs, and the like).†

Viewed praxially, then, "music" is not merely an added *accompaniment* to or a secondary or minor component of an otherwise nonmusical social praxis, such as religion or nationalism (though it serves those social needs). Instead, it is a central ingredient, differently created *for* and *by* the particular socio-musical praxis at stake. So, for example, religious music is not just an entertaining diversion in a religious service; it is a key form of prayer or worship praxis that also helps establish a reverent state of mind. A concert of whatever kind of music, then, is not just a random grouping of people; it is 'for' their collective musical interests and dispositions. Whatever they find musically pleasurable (depending on the type of music) is why they are there and what they socially share. Their 'being together' for the music is, then, evidence of sociality served through music.

As regards religious music, for example, notice differences between the music of a folk mass and a Palestrina mass or between a hymn or chorale and gospel choir singing. And concerts feature music for audience listening, the sociality of which varies between musics (e.g., 'classical' concerts, jazz heard in a club, rock concerts, and the like). Some marriage ceremonies take place without music, but a wedding in which music is central to the ceremonial praxis—especially where it has been carefully chosen by the couple—significantly contributes to the *meaning* of the ceremony in combination with the vows and other features of the wedding service.

Consider, also, the role of music in sociopolitical events: the musically inspired revolutions in, for example, Estonia† or Chile, where governments have fallen because of musical forms of resistance to a regime. In fact, totalitarian regimes try mightily to govern or suppress certain musics because they want to subdue such social influences—for example, the suppression of the compositions of Shostakovich in Russia under Stalin. Other regimes promote musics that support government political values—for example, the music of Wagner and Bruckner under Hitler.†

For praxialism, then, even music that is intended to be 'good for' *audience listening*, such as 'classical' music, jazz, and 'popular' musics, is also thoroughly imbued with *four social attributes* that condition its sounding forms. First, social meanings are *always* involved, such as the social symbolism* (i.e., semiotics) contributed by the spaces and places in which music is performed—for example, a jazz concert heard in a church (which happens) or (more typically) music with religious texts heard in a secular concert hall, or the different audience behavior and dress according to the type of music (e.g., the difference between the behavior of a 'classical' concert audience and the audience at a rock or jazz concert).

Second, music functions culturally as a social text.* Thus, for example, various social meanings inhere in music (everything from the instruments used to the different rationality of tonal and serial music used in various musical systems, such as those in the East and in the West). Moreover, social meanings—such as gender roles* and especially social class—are read into and from it.

13

Third, it activates the socializing effects of *interactional synchrony*—where minds are collectively 'tuned' to or harmonized by the music—the 'affective being together' where affective states are shared by audience members, often very differently according to different kinds of music.*† Think, for example, if you were alone for a performance of, say, Beethoven's *Ninth Symphony*; you would miss in many ways the social essence of the musical experience. (In audio recording, a change of philosophy has taken place in recent decades from when a single mic was placed centrally, as though a perfectly situated listener. Today, this has been replaced by multitrack recordings that presume to present someone's notion of an ideal balance. This 'performing' of the music by recording engineers and other variables of the recording industry give evidence of the social role of musicking.) The contribution of the concert audience to one's experience of "the music," including the acoustics of where one sits, is missing in recorded music (although such listening is socially saturated in other ways).†

And finally, music also has a host of other down-to-earth social attributes and values (e.g., the social foundations of music in sociology,* various musical apps, national and ethnic musics) that aesthetic theorists have denied or denigrated because they contradict noble-sounding aesthetic theories of "pure" and cerebral music. Not surprisingly, then, the music of nationalist composers is highly favored in their home nations. But, as a result of the aesthetic theory of music, where such associations are said to be "extra-musical," only the compositions of composers of international repute reach the world stage—that is, for the pleasures of other audiences, as "absolute music."† Try arguing that with those who listen with great admiration to the music of national composers not otherwise recognized in most of the rest of the world.

By ignoring these four social attributes of all kinds of concert music (and the social conditions that support nonconcert music), the sociological, ethnomusicological, anthropological, and analyses from cultural studies of the central social role of music in helping create what we know as society, culture, and the so-called *"social mind"*†—all these studies are typically excluded from the student's studies. Think about, for example, how "natural" gamelan music is for Indonesians or Kabuki music to Japanese—yet how odd and musically and socially meaningless it is for those not immersed in the cultural context. These factors go well beyond "contextualist" defenses of the aesthetic theory of art and music* that speculate on but fail to agree as to whether such social, practical, cultural, and "extra-musical" contexts can properly be part of the aesthetic 'content' of music.

Thus, for the most part, music is studied as what is called *absolute music*, as though fully 'for itself'—notes in relation to other notes.† However, the lack of acknowledgment of the role of these many sociocultural dimensions in musical meaning and experience creates an especially major challenge for praxial music education in its attempts to recognize and promote the *living* value of music for society and individuals. The aesthetic ideology thus continues to prevent music teachers from understanding and teaching in terms of praxial evidence that music is broadly and properly understood as a valued social praxis.

The result in recent years has been the need for ever more advocacy to promote the benefits of music education to voters (and educational authorities) who, had they personally experienced the claimed aesthetic benefits of school music during their own schooling, would presumably support school music.† School music instead ends up as a minor and small island of music, lasting only for the school years and set off from the very vibrant world of music outside school. And, in the competition for students' affections, interests, and long-term commitments, the aesthetic rationale for music education has clearly been fighting a losing battle. Thus, there exists a mounting sense on the part of the public of the irrelevance of school music to graduates' lives and society and, in the long run, to voters' support for it. School budget votes and the erosion of the number of music teachers (or ever larger classes) in school programs demonstrate the uncomfortable reality created by the aesthetic ideology.†

. . .

The analysis in Chapter Two of a philosophy of praxialism in music and music education begins with a critical account of the rise of the speculative-rationalist aesthetic theory of art and the aesthetic *ideology* only two centuries ago. It is this ideology that needs to be critically reconsidered, from the perspectives of both the philosophy of music and music education. It has gone unchallenged for too long in music education (though roundly challenged elsewhere).†

For purposes of this critical history, there are (at least) two meanings of the term "ideology."† The most general and neutral sense is in reference to a *system of ideas* that organizes institutional, social, and personal conduct—for example, the institutions of schooling, banking, and law. These, however, are always qualified by their social contexts; for example, all three are often vastly different in various countries.

In what follows here, however, the concept of ideology is influenced by the social philosophy of Critical Theory. For *critical social theory** (and Critical Pedagogy in educational theory†), the term "ideology" refers to the efforts of a *dominant* sociocultural (and often economic) group—dominant in terms of its power and authority, not size—to advance—even, if needed, to impose—its values over those of less dominant groups, whether or not they approve. In this sense, an ideology—unlike references to it in the general and neutral sense—can be a critically important social problem; such ideology is something to be overcome, to be emancipated from.

Aesthetic theory as propagated by aesthetes and cognoscenti, and into which music teachers are thoroughly socialized in their university studies, can reasonably be—and has definitely been*—regarded as such an imposed, imposing, and dominating ideology. Studies of the social roles of music in society and culture that contradict the aesthetic creed are therefore simply excluded from such studies in universities and schools. And, as thereby

15

firmly embedded in the minds of music teachers, the influence of the aesthetic ideology is difficult for music teachers to escape—especially if they don't recognize its symptoms because of their all-encompassing social *indoctrination* into the ideology that was the taken-for-granted, singular premise of their musical studies. (Readers might well consider what other social ideologies of this kind they have been indoctrinated into and have thus taken for granted. Romantic love? Capitalism? Religion? Politics? Gender identities? "Culture shock" is a result of encountering uncomfortable differences between ideologies.)

The *ideology critique* that follows (Part One) is undertaken mainly from within the accounts of analytic philosophy itself. But it also draws on findings from the sociology of music, social psychology, cultural studies, social philosophy, cultural anthropology, cultural studies, and practice theory that most music theorists, historians, and musicians are unaware of or mistakenly dismiss as "extra-musical" and therefore irrelevant. This *musica practica* is often ignored both in the histories of music taught and in accounts of music's social role and importance to the everyday choices of millions of people. The problems of the speculative-rationalist aesthetic ideology as a basis or rationale for music education are then evaluated in Chapter Three.

Then, in Part Two, the advantages of a praxial philosophy of music and music education, called Action Learning,† are proposed as a remedy for the problems of the aesthetic claims made by teachers in support (or defense) of their teaching. And the text concludes with a challenge for music teachers to promote the benefits of "breaking 100 in music."† I hope this action ideal† will become clear as an easily remembered motto for guiding music teaching as praxis—the guiding ideal of 'turning on' students to music as a lifelong enrichment.

Related Readings

(Annotated, except where the title is a clear reference to the content.)

Clare Saunders, David Mossley, George MacDonald Ross, and Danielle Lamb (with Julie Closs). *Doing Philosophy: A Practical Guide for Students.* London: Continuum, 2007.
For the quotation opening this chapter, see p. 3.

Jean-François Lyotard. *Why Philosophize?* Cambridge: Polity Press, 2013.
On the essential role of philosophy as a transformative force in the modern world.

Irving Singer. *Philosophy of Love.* Cambridge, MA: MIT Press, 2011.
Dare you read it?

Berit Brogaard. *On Romantic Love.* New York: Oxford University Press, 2015.
A new philosophy of love.

Neil Gascoigne and Tim Thornton. *Tacit Knowledge.* Bristol CN: Acumen, 2013.
Important differences between knowledge for 'doing' vs. knowledge 'about'. Discussions later in this text about 'music appreciation' rely on this distinction!

Denis Dutton. *The Art Instinct*. New York: Bloomsbury, 2009.
Art as a natural and evolutionary endowment that creates culture.

Georgina Born and David Hesmondhalgh, eds. *Western Music and Its Others: Difference, Representation, and Appropriation in Music*. Berkeley: University of California Press, 2000.
How music creates sociocultural identities and cultural difference: race, gender, and so on.

Ellen Dissanayake. *Art and Intimacy: How the Arts Began*. Seattle: University of Washington Press, 2000.
A study from cultural anthropology of the common evolutionary origins of art and love.

Janet Wolff. *The Social Production of Art*. New York: New York University Press, 1984.
On the sociology of art.

Vera L. Zolberg. *Constructing a Sociology of the Arts*. Cambridge: Cambridge University Press, 1990.
Totally ignored in the training of music teachers.

Peter J. Martin. *Music and the Sociological Gaze: Art Worlds and Cultural Production*. Manchester: Manchester University Press, 2006.
By a leading sociologist of music.

Julia Eklund Koza. "Listening for Whiteness: Hearing Racial Politics in Undergraduate School Music." In T. A. Regelski and J. T. Gates, eds., *Music Education for Changing Times: Guiding Visions for Practice*. New York: Springer, 2009; 85–96.
A critique of racial politics used in admission standards.

Wayne Bowman, ed. *Action, Criticism, and Theory for Music Education*. Special issue on race, music, and music education; http://act.maydaygroup.org/articles/Bowman4_3.pdf (accessed May 15, 2015).

Elizabeth Gould. "Dis-orientations of Desire: Music Education Queer." In T. A. Regelski and J. T. Gates, eds., *Music Education for Changing Times: Guiding Visions for Practice*. New York: Springer, 2009; 59–72.
Music education and queer theory.

Brian Roberts, ed. *Action, Criticism, and Theory for Music Education*. Special issue on music and identity; http://act.maydaygroup.org/articles/Roberts9_2.pdf (accessed May 15, 2015).

Noël Carroll. *A Philosophy of Mass Art*. Oxford: Clarendon Press, 1998.
An important account and critique of the "aesthetic theory of art": 89–109.

Thomas A. Regelski. "Praxialism and 'Aesthetic This, Aesthetic That, Aesthetic Whatever'." *Action, Criticism, and Theory for Music Education* 10(2): 61–99; http://act.maydaygroup.org/articles/Regelski10_2.pdf (accessed May 15, 2015).
A pointed philosophical critique of the aesthetic ideology against the philosopher who first introduced the term "praxis."

Thomas A. Regelski. "Curriculum: Implications of Aesthetic versus Praxial Philosophies." In D. J. Elliott, ed., *Praxial Music Education: Reflections and Dialogues*. New York: Oxford University Press, 2005; 219–248.
An exploration of the curricular differences between the two.

David J. Elliott, ed. *Praxial Music Education: Reflections and Dialogues.* New York: Oxford University Press, 2005.
An important collection of different praxial philosophies (replied to online by Elliott).

David Cooper, ed. *A Companion to Aesthetics.* Oxford: Blackwell, 1999.
A reference work for understanding aesthetics; dictionary style (with author citations) and easy to use.

Berys Gaut and Dominic McIver Lopes, eds. *The Routledge Companion to Aesthetics.* London: Routledge, 2001.
One author per topic; yet another reference work needed to understand aesthetics.

Peter Kivy, ed. *The Blackwell Guide to Aesthetics.* Oxford: Blackwell, 2004.
Still another reference (one author per topic). Apparently the earlier volumes (those listed here and many others not listed), were not enough to resolve differences among aestheticians.

Jean-Marie Schaeffer. *Art of the Modern Age: Philosophy of Art from Kant to Heidegger.* Trans. S. Rendall. Princeton: Princeton University Press, 2000.
An important critical history of the "spectatorship" theory of art. Any objections to criticism of aesthetic theory need to contend with the argument and scholarship of this seminal study. Note the title: "philosophy of art," not "aesthetics of art."

Peter Kivy. *Music Alone: Philosophical Reflections on the Purely Musical Experience.* Ithaca: Cornell University Press, 1990.
A defense of "absolute music" (instrumental music without words). The author doesn't intend to offend lovers of choral music and song, but you can make up your own mind.

Lawrence W. Levine. *Highbrow/Lowbrow: The Emergence of Cultural Hierarchy in America.* Cambridge, MA: Harvard University Press.
A classic study of cultural history in the United States in relation to social class. Important!

Richard A. Peterson. and Roger M. Kern. "Changing Highbrow Taste: From Snob to Omnivore." *American Sociological Review* 61 (October 1996): 900–907.
Sociological research on the tastes of otherwise snobbish highbrow listeners.

Philip Alperson. "What Should One Expect from a Philosophy of Music Education?" *Journal of Aesthetic Education* 25(3) (Fall 1991): 215–229.
A comparison of different aesthetic theories of music and an argument for the need to consider all music praxis.

Philip Alperson. "Music Education." In T. Gracyk and A. Kania, eds., *The Routledge Companion to Philosophy and Music.* New York: Routledge, 2014; 614–623.
A shorter version of the previous citation in which the author (mistakenly) takes credit for inventing praxialism.

T. R. Schatzki, K. Cetina, and E. V Savigny, eds. *The Practice Turn in Contemporary Theory.* London: Routledge, 2001.
Groundbreaking philosophy of "practice theory."

Theodore R. Schatzki. *Social Practices: A Wittgensteinian Approach to Human Activity and the Social.* Cambridge: Cambridge University Press, 1996.
About social practice as fundamental to individuality, and a pragmatic philosophy of meaning as use.

Etienne Wenger. *Communities of Practice: Learning, Meaning, and Identity.* Cambridge: Cambridge University Press, 1999.
A community of practice is a social context that gives structure, meaning, and identity to our lives. 'Must' reading in practice theory.

Marie McCarthy, ed. *Music Education as Praxis.* College Park: University of Maryland Press, 1999.
A diverse collection of important essays on praxial themes.

David J. Elliott. *Music Matters: A New Philosophy of Music Education.* New York: Oxford University Press, 1994.
The first philosophy of the new (nonaesthetic) philosophy of praxialism in music education.

David J. Elliot and Marissa Silverman. *Music Matters: A Philosophy of Music Education,* 2nd ed. New York: Oxford University Press, 2015.
A major updating of the previous edition (the previous citation). Much more supportive research.

David Elliott. *Praxial Music Education: Reflections and Dialogues.* New York: Oxford University Press, 2005.
Responses by various praxialists to Elliott's 1994 book (cited earlier).

Theodore R. Schatzki. *The Site of the Social.* University Park: Pennsylvania State University Press, 2002.
A seminal treatise on "practice theory."

Eviatar Zerubavel. *Social Mindscapes: An Invitation to Cognitive Sociology.* Cambridge, MA: Harvard University Press, 1997.
The cognitive bases of the social mind.

On Dalcroze *eurhythmics,* a praxis of the bodily bases of music, see: http://www.dalcrozeusa.org/ (accessed May 15, 2015).

F. J. Varela, E. Thompson, and E. Rosch, eds. *The Embodied Mind: Cognitive Science and Human Experiences.* Cambridge, MA: MIT Press, 1991.
About the bodily bases of the mind.

Mark Johnson. *The Body in the Mind: The Bodily Basis of Meaning, Imagination, and Reason.* Chicago: University of Chicago Press, 1987.
On 'minding' the body: the mind in the body and the body in the mind.

Pentti Määttänen. "Semiotics of Space: Peirce and Lefebvre." *Semiotics* 1(4) (2007): 453–461.
Spaces often have social symbolism: a church, a concert hall, a public park.

Juha Ojala. *Space in Musical Semiosis.* Imatra: Semiotic Society of Finland, 2009.
A semiotic study of musical composition rooted in pragmatism and praxial criteria.

John Shepherd. *Music as Social Text.* Cambridge: Polity Press, 1991.
The social meanings in and from music.

Max Weber. *The Rational and Social Foundations of Music.* Trans. D. Martindale, J. Riedel, and G. Neuwirth. Carbondale: Southern Illinois University Press, 1969.
How music's rational properties (e.g., scales, harmony, notation) are rooted in Western social institutions.

William Benzon. *Beethoven's Anvil: Music in Mind and Culture*. New York: Basic Books, 2001.
About "interactional synchrony" and other interesting aspects of music in relation to culture and mind: 25–29, 41–42.

Philippe Rochat. *Others in Mind: Social Origins of Self-Consciousness*. Cambridge: Cambridge University Press, 2009.
The social effects of others on our minds.

David Davies. "Medium." In T. Gracyk and A. Kania, *The Routledge Companion to Philosophy and Music*. New York: Routledge, 2014.
About the futile attempts of aesthetic "contextualism" to qualify aesthetic experience: 56–58.

Ben Agger. *Critical Social Theories: An Introduction*. Boulder, CO: Westview Press, 1998.

Craig Calhoun. *Critical Social Theory*. Oxford: Blackwell, 1995.

1

MUSICA PRACTICA COMPARED TO AESTHETIC SPECULATIONS

There are two musics. . . : the music one listens to, the music one plays. . . .

*The music one plays come from an activity that is very little auditory, being above all manuat [sic] (and thus in a way much more sensual). It is the music which you or I can play, alone, or among friends, with no other audience than its participants. . . . This music has disappeared; initially the province of the idle (aristocratic) class, it lapsed into an insipid social rite with the coming of the democracy of the bourgeoisie (the piano, the young lady, the drawing room, the nocturne) and then faded out altogether (who plays the piano today?). To find practical music in the West, one has now to look to another public, another repertoire, another instrument. . . . Concurrently, passive, receptive music, sound music, is [sic] become **the** music (that of concert, festival, record, radio): playing has ceased to exist. So too has the performer changed. The amateur, a role defined much more by a style than by a technical imperfection, is no longer anywhere to be found; the professionals, pure specialists whose training remains entirely esoteric for the public (who is there who is still acquainted with the problems of music education?), never offer that style of the perfect amateur . . ., touching off in us not satisfaction but desire, the desire to **make** that music. . . . In short, there was first the actor of music, then the interpreter (the grand Romantic voice), then finally the technician, who relieves the listener of all activity, even by procuration, and abolishes in the sphere of music the very notion of **doing**.*

Roland Barthes, *"Musica Practica"**

Recent contributions to aesthetics . . . have done little to dispel the charge of dreariness and irrelevance that has hung over the subject throughout its brief history. The familiar and the obvious are the first casualties in philosophical discussion: thus aesthetic theory often seems false to our experience of art. . . . Recently, such an inadequacy to our experience of art has been evident; a result, I believe, partly of aesthetician's preoccupation with what it is to

21

treat something 'aesthetically', and partly from a concentration on works of art in isolation from the circumstances in which they are actually created or appreciated.

Michael Proudfoot*

This chapter describes how music as we know it today changed from being *respected* as a matter-of-fact social *praxis* serving a variety of everyday social needs, doings, and uses—*musica practica*—to a rarefied *theory* of 'fine art' based on aesthetic theories that arose in the mid-eighteenth century on *rational* foundations inherited from the seventeenth-century Age of Reason. Of course, as shall be recapped from time to time, despite this aesthetic rationale and the social rite of the public concert that it led to, music in the world today—including concert music—is still always praxial.† But its praxial attributes and values get almost entirely set aside in schools and universities by the dominance of the development, in 1750, of 'modern' aesthetic theories (explained later).

The historical scrutiny of the aesthetic theory of art and music that follows is thus gauged to inform the reader that praxis is not some newfangled idea and that it has a long and distinguished history; *musica practica* predates aesthetic theory by thousands of years. Even today, the social evidence of music as praxis outweighs in every respect the reverence given by aesthetic theories to only a very small percentage of all the music in the world—mostly from the nineteenth and the first half of the twentieth centuries. As will be argued, discarding the understanding of music as praxis—as *musica practica*—was not progress in the history of ideas.

. . .

The Invention of 'Fine Art'—from Aisthesis to Aesthetics

Among the historic reasons for the rise of the idea of 'fine art' are philosophical precedents from ancient Greece† that began to be applied to the arts in the mid-fifteenth to early sixteenth centuries.* That era was characterized by a revival of classical Greek learning—the Renaissance (from the Latin *renascens*, "to be born again")—that replaced the religious austerity and scholastic philosophy of the late Middle Ages.

(An aside of potential interest to today's students and teachers: Today's "scholars" get their status and title from medieval "scholasticism" and its defense, based on Aristotelian logic, of Catholic theology. Another continuing debt to that distant age is the medieval caps and gowns of graduation exercises and the *lecture method*. The need to lecture was dictated by the conditions of a wandering scholar, in the days before publishing, who had one handwritten copy of his and—in those days it was *his*—"thesis" and who held forth and "professed" it for students and others. He was assisted in "defending" his thesis against other scholars with the help of "masters" (students who had "mastered" his thesis)—called "bachelors" for the obvious reason that they were free to roam with the "professor" in behalf of his thesis. The geographical crossroads of these "professions" and "defenses" of scholarly theses became the sites of the first European universities.)

Much of medieval scholasticism, it seems, remains today. Consider, for example, students' complaints that their studies are "merely academic," thus harkening back to Plato's philosophy that "ideal forms" (i.e., ideas and abstract concepts) were more 'real' (universal: the idea(l) of "chair") than the 'things' of the empirical world (the different shapes of actual chairs). His idealism was taught in the Academy, named after the war hero Academus and hence the source of the expression "merely academic" (i.e., teaching abstract ideas rather than addressing the 'real world'). One of Plato's students was Aristotle, who disagreed with his teacher by according respect to knowledge of empirical 'things' (via aisthesis).† Today, terms such as "scholar," "school," and "scholarship" are all derived from scholasticism rooted in Aristotelian thinking as understood by the medieval age. But in much of schooling today, Plato's *idealism* tends to overshadow Aristotle's *realism*. Even much of the science in schools teaches the findings of classical experiments as factual ideas, rather than instructing from a praxial perspective of actually 'doing' science.

In the era of the Renaissance in Western Europe (late fourteenth to late sixteenth century), there arose a humanist ideal concerning the full development and flourishing of individual potentiality. For Renaissance *humanism*, "man is the measure of all things"—a saying credited to the Greek philosopher Protagoras (c. 485 B.C.–415 B.C.). This new emphasis on human worth and dignity helped foster the idea of the *individual* as a highly distinct or unique Self. Renaissance artists, authors, and composers thus no longer saw themselves as anonymous artisans and began take personal credit for their creations by signing them.†

However, as throughout prior Western (and much of world) history, all of the Renaissance arts continued to be praxial; the music recounted in today's history books, for example, continued to be closely wed to its functional role in religion and the royal and princely courts and thus in the social lives of nobles, courtiers, and the aristocracy. Even the music of the rising middle class—the bourgeoisie—was functional; it demonstrated the wealth and class of this rising class. (Music in the everyday lives of 'commoners' is mainly ignored or avoided by traditional musicologists, except for the music of troubadours, trouveres, and minnesingers in the history of song.) Eventually, *polyphony*, with its multiple "voices" performing the same (or sometimes different) texts at different times, gave way to *homophony* (a melody supported by chords). Texts thus became more comprehensible, and melodies, harmonies, and rhythms could be wed to textual meaning (and forms) and their emotional impact on listeners considered. This trend was central to the beginnings of opera—itself an attempt to recreate what the Camerata, an influential group of Renaissance musicians, noblemen, and intellectuals, believed (mistakenly) to be the expressive power of music in ancient Greek drama. (Music in ancient Greece was almost entirely vocal and largely identified with the spoken words of literary forms.*)

In addition, the "courtly love" of the Middle Ages, as predicated on the neoplatonic idea(l)—"Platonic love"—of a knight serving his courtly lady, evolved musically into the typically sentimental love themes of Renaissance madrigals. Among other influences, these helped give social impetus to the modern concept of *romantic love*. This concept was quite new at the time (at least as regards common social discourse and terminology). It was also tied to the evolving concept of the individual and the states of mind experienced by individuals, and it is a source of today's popular love songs.

There was also new interest in *nature* as a result of the rediscovery of Aristotle's writings. Aristotle's realism (unlike Plato's idealism) took an active interest in the external world. Accordingly, he valued *aisthesis*: *empirical knowledge gained via the senses.*† This empiricism inspired the scientific revolution in the sixteenth and seventeenth centuries, and, as a result, important roots in the history of science stem from this period (e.g., Galileo, Copernicus, Newton).*

Accordingly, visual artists also began to include *nature* as an important subject of its own in addition to depicting religious themes and portraits of famous individuals. Along with love themes, then, topics from nature also entered the madrigal and song literature and eventually became a staple of the Western repertory of art song and lied. Such vocal music, of course, depends on words that unavoidably have "extra-musical" references (concepts referred to by words: e.g., the evolving language of love) and thus *socially rooted meanings.*† The rising focus on the individual increasingly led to states of mind that experienced the themes of both love and nature in new and important arts-related ways. The arts, as social activities, thus helped mediate the evolving Western concept of individual Selves in interaction, often via art and music.

In particular, certain psychological language about the personal and affective (or 'feelingful') aspects of an individual's experiences in any realm increasingly came into vogue.† The functional (i.e., praxial) nature of the arts was, if anything, thus strengthened by language that acknowledged and referred to the potent effects of such affective experiences.* In short, the arts were effective or powerful as praxis because of their highly attractive affective *aisthesic* qualities, thus revealing the appealing traits (in Latin, *qualia*) of sensory knowledge over the abstractions of reason.

Over time, aisthesis had thus become a particular kind of sensibility or *sensory appeal* associated with the visual arts and music.† As a result, by the late Renaissance the idea of the 'fine arts' began to evolve. Thus, as a 'fine art', "music" (as a collective noun for "music*s*": "music" is to "musics" as "food" is to "foods") gradually was divorced from any particular social praxis and became increasingly featured in concerts and recitals that were set aside from daily life—*though no less social.*†

Thus, performing and even concert listening involved (then as now) clearly social praxis.* Moreover, the ideas and emotions experienced by an individual (artistic or otherwise) are social in their origins and ramifications. This sociality accounts for differences in the musics of various cultures and subcultures. In other words, what individuals respond to emotionally and how (or in what ways) they respond are unavoidably influenced by and even learned through sociality. There are, of course, certain 'hardwired' emotional states, such as the fear of "fight or flight" responses. But otherwise the range of daily emotions is socially determined.* Consider, for example, the different cultural reactions to and rites for death. (In rural China and Taiwan, for example, striptease dancers are often hired to perform at funerals in order to attract more 'mourners'.*)

By the eighteenth century, developments in Europe associated with the Age of Reason and the Enlightenment† (especially the rationalism discussed later) began to merge the long and diverse history of Western theorizing about music into the speculative-rationalistic *aesthetic theory of art* introduced in the previous chapter.* This kind of theorizing not only attempted to *replace* the universal praxialism of previous centuries; it sought also to *reject* it in favor of the "spectatorship theory" of art and music rooted solely in the leisure-time contemplation of the newly rising middle class! This "invention of art"* was, of course, a socially created value based largely on the social sources and promotion of the new aesthetic theory.

The social value of art and concert music for the new and affluent middle class (the bourgeoisie, not workers) was its *practical uselessness.** Its major social function (though still involving important sociality) was not much more than to exhibit conspicuous wealth and social prestige, thereby serving middle-class aspirations to aristocratic status. And the concert etiquette that arose in connection with the aesthetic theory of music—as enforced by musical patrons and concert societies (usually the same rich connoisseurs)—progressively denied the bodily (somatic) bases of musical responding and experience.* Thus, audiences instead were trained to sit silently still, as though in church,† and to contemplate music cerebrally.*

Audience members were, in effect, supposed to be entirely engrossed in their own minds, as though alone—even though socially together. Even the very evident social dimensions of concert attendance, behavior, and interactions were thereby denied relevance (e.g., dress codes, intermission socializing, applause, pre- and postconcert discussions, music criticism, concert hall design).† One reason for the attractions of 'popular' music concerts may be the abandonment of such obsessively formal audience etiquette and the restoration of the role of the body in musical responding.*

Autonomous Music as Divorced from Everyday Life

The concept of musical *autonomy* arose in the late eighteenth and nineteenth centuries when the other "sister arts" (painting, sculpture, literature) were being strictly regarded in aesthetic terms as "pure"—what aestheticians call "absolute music": abstract instrumental music 'free' of the connection of words with or programmatic references to 'real life'.* Thus, "art for art's sake" *aestheticism* became the leading premise early in the Romantic era in music history: the doctrine that art and music exist for the contemplation of beauty alone (or the "sublime" in nineteenth-century art theory, discussed later) and that it need no longer serve social themes, needs, and practices (*musica practica*), what aesthetician Peter Kivy favorably describes as the "liberation of music" from worldly toil and suffering.* The onset of concertgoing also saw the rise of the cult of the *virtuoso* (e.g., Paganini, Liszt), the triumph of the concept of *genius* (e.g., Beethoven), and the rise of music *impresarios* (in the United States, e.g., John Philip Sousa, P. T. Barnum), and it was a prime focus of the Chautauqua Movement of the late nineteenth and early twentieth centuries in the United States.*

Thus began a social trend to what, in the early twentieth century, the music sociologist and social critic Theodor W. Adorno (also a champion of Schoenberg) regarded as the *commodification* of art and music. His complaint was that art and music had become commodities—mere 'things'—for sale under the rising influence of capitalism and the commercial 'art world' business. Thus, he argued, *artistic* ideals had been challenged by *economic* considerations, such as getting published, performed, and recognized and the whole range of economic interests that replaced musical integrity.* (In short, we see the rise of today's 'classical' music *industry* with symphony orchestras, opera companies, and virtuoso soloists competing for the economic limelight at a time when audiences are dwindling. The rise of 'popular' music praxis either further complicated this critique of commodification or confirmed it.)

As one result, 'good music' was increasingly (and intentionally) distanced from the important social conditions and functions that that bring it into being, that is, from the many pragmatic, down-to-earth conditions, needs, uses, and functions that aestheticism regarded as impure, debasing, or limiting. Thus arose the idea of absolute music as thoroughly—and, according to aesthetes, properly—divorced from the "extra-musical" relations, contexts, and functions that always have always elicited and characterized it. In other words, it was divorced from everyday life and relegated to special and rare times of leisure use: concerts, recitals, and (today) listening to recordings.†

Accordingly, consuming music as a 'fine art' became a sign of re*fine*ment. As is commonly thought, "there is a kind of common-sense sociology of music familiar to us all. We know that, generally, fine art is for fine people and vulgar art is for the not so fine."* *Classic*al music was thereby associated with 'classy' taste and conspicuous highbrow cultural consumption.† This status 'above' ordinary life raised it to almost metaphysical heights, thus further separating it from everyday life. All these contributing conditions and ideas, of course, are themselves completely and essentially social and thus unavoidably "extra-musical." However, the many *social sources of aestheticist ideology* in behalf of the "pure gaze" of responding to art were (and still are) themselves mindfully overlooked or denied in exalting the personal responses of individual listeners.* Yet, in the meanwhile, musics of all kinds continue to this day to perform their praxial functions in ways that are defining of society and the culture of daily life.

This important social element of music in history has been largely ignored by traditional musicologists and music theorists in favor of the aesthetic theory of musical meaning and value that studies musical scores analytically in a way that, in effect, is often *an*esthetizing. Thus, the academic study of music in conservatories and schools of music (a consequence of the Enlightenment's contribution to the scientific claims of scholarly disciplines, such as musicology and music theory) has accounted almost exclusively for 'high' or 'art music'. The vast preponderance of other musics and musical practices (not to mention 'popular' musics, and ethnic musics of the non-Western world) have thus been studiously ignored (or dismissed with colonialist arrogance). In universities that even occasionally offer such studies they are usually elective, not basic enough to be required.

Music has been regarded as important in history enough that it had been studied formally since at least Pythagoras. In the Medieval and Renaissance universities it was taught as part of the *quadrivium* (arithmetic, geometry, *musica theoretica*, and astronomy) in preparation for the advanced study of philosophy, and *musica practica* was among the studies (the *trivium*) for deriving reliable knowledge from the senses (aisthesis). However, today's typical theory, history, and 'music appreciation' textbooks and classes typically address only an incredibly small percentage of all the music in the world—even of the Western world—certainly not the musics used and enjoyed daily by most people. That fact alone is ample evidence of the aesthetic ideology at work in socializing and indoctrinating music teachers. Why, given the ample evidence of the importance of music in social contexts, is that praxial role studiously eliminated from the education of teacher educators? (Do you risk asking that question of a music history professor?)

Music theory, for its part, has been concerned only with the relation of pitches to other pitches—with abstractions of form, structure, analysis—not with the situated conditions, practices, and occasions in which music is typically used, heard, and enjoyed. Similarly, music history has typically studied the relation of leading composers and their compositions to what preceded and followed them. It has attempted to follow the 'development' or evolution of 'art' music over time (as though the imagined 'progress' of musical 'development' in history follows some kind of scientific law)* and, thus, to empirically account for differences in styles, eras, and between composers.

One result has been that many musicians and music educators believe (small "p")† that the way they have been taught to listen—analytically, to formal and stylistic features and "aesthetic properties"—is the proper and only mode of what is called 'music appreciation'.† In fact, the claim has also been made* that music is best 'heard' inwardly, intellectually, only by studying scores, and that those who have to actually listen to music being performed were limited

to listening only viscerally or emotionally, as a mere entertainment or amusement. And, of course, leading composers of music of the late twentieth and the early twenty-first centuries give little credence to musical criteria advanced by nineteenth-century aesthetic theories. And they pay no attention to attempts to account for their musics in terms of the aesthetic theory of art and music.†
(Were John Cage alive, it seems predictable that he would have be amused by the rationalizations made by aestheticians about his later compositions (e.g., *3'44'* of silence)—since he had a good sense of humor. And despite aesthetician's concern to provide aesthetic rationales for very recent music, Cage influenced many composers to consider ideas far outside the aesthetic creed).*

The rise of this gap between music, life, and ordinary people was directly influenced by the *rationalism* that the eighteenth-century Enlightenment inherited from the seventeenth-century Age of Reason. And the gap was especially widened by the corresponding separation of mind and body by the philosophical dualism of Renaissance philosopher René Descartes (1596–1650). Descartes is sometimes known as the 'father' of modern philosophy, and he laid the basis for seventeenth-century rationalism. For Descartes, the 'mind' was distinct from the physical 'brain', and thus the role of the physical body (aisthesis) was trivialized in favor of reason. The legacy of this separation results in the lack of proper acknowledgment by aesthetic theory of the embodied bases of music making and responding.* But, Descartes's dualism is widely rejected by today's philosophy and neuroscience.*

However, in advancing the new scientific method, the Enlightenment also advanced *empiricism* (along the lines of Aristotle's acknowledgment of aisthesis). One result was the just-mentioned origination of the disciplines of musicology and music theory. Both claim to follow a scientific model in attempting to analyze musical 'works' as though they were free-standing *stimulus objects* that carry intrinsic and thus supposedly timeless, placeless, and faceless aesthetic meanings, values, and truths—as though studying a peacock's feathers as beautiful. This has led to what one sociologist of music describes as "the intellectual retardedness of positivistic musicology"—positivism, in this case, referring to the scientific models of traditional musicology.* (What is called the "new musicology"* is, in contrast, deeply concerned with social themes and interpretations.)

This 'objectification' of music praxis into 'works' of 'art' (on the model of the visual arts and literature that produce 'things')* had long since been advanced by the invention, in 1501, of music printing. By the end of the Renaissance, the publishing industry was well under way. As physical objects, scores were bought and sold (or borrowed or rented), and "the music"—understood as notes on a page†—became all the more associated with 'works' rather than with the many and varied sociocultural uses to which music—notated or not—was still put.

Such published 'works' of music could also be collected in libraries and studied and analyzed 'scientifically' and rationally, thus giving rise to the discipline of music theory at the hands of Jean-Philippe Rameau and his successors. The resulting "common practice" theory now taught in schools and universities, however, is far from what is common praxis in the various musics of our day—popular or contemporary 'art' musics—and thus bears little or no relation to *musica practica*. Newer aesthetic theories also have little or no relevance to the music of contemporary composers.

In the philosophical debates inherited from the Greeks, of particular interest for the arts (and the history of science) have been the continuous attempts of philosophers to account for knowledge gained through the senses. As mentioned earlier in this chapter,† this was the original Greek meaning of the term *aisthesis* from which the term "aesthetics" was derived and from which aesthetic theory has progressively deviated. Plato notoriously distrusted the senses.

But his student Aristotle attributed an important cognitive value to the senses and empirical knowledge (e.g., "seeing is believing").† However, aisthesis was not regarded (then, or up through the eighteenth century) as rational or trustworthy—mainly because it dwelled on and thus was relative to the *unique particulars* of an individual's distinctive sensory experience. The rationalist critique was that sensory experience was processed differently by different bodies. Thus, it failed to result in the *abstract universals* that the (supposedly) 'higher' faculty of reason was believed to reveal. Because people perceived things differently (given different bodies and experiences), aisthesis was thus regarded as an inferior source of 'subjective' knowledge in comparison to the fruits of logical reasoning, which were believed to be 'objective', universal, and true for all times, people, and places (e.g., Aristotle's *theoria*, explained in Chapter Six).† Despite the frequent use of artistic metaphors of "taste," even the senses were ranked, with the 'higher' senses being sight and hearing, the 'lower' senses being touch, taste, and smell.

Nonetheless, the recognition and expression of inward, personal sensibility that had become more common with the Renaissance became increasingly common in reference to art and music.† It led eventually to the concept of refined "taste" (i.e., for beauty) that eventually developed from the speculative-rationalist aesthetic theory of art.* Ever since, the idea of 'good taste' has been a contentious issue.

In particular, the concept of aisthesis led to the attempts of the German philosopher Alexander Baumgarten to *legitimate judgments of sense* (aisthesis) in relation to art in terms more favorable to the prevailing rationalism of his student days. However, Baumgarten's sole focus was poetry, and, with the *Aesthetica* of 1750, his literary model was indiscriminately generalized to the other arts (despite the obviously major differences in media and artistic praxis). It then gave the new field of study the name "aesthetics" and provided the foundations for the aesthetic theory of 'fine art' and 'good taste' that survive to this day.

Baumgarten's proposed new "science," as he considered it, was to be to sensuous knowledge what logic and reason are to rational knowledge. The intent, thus, was to make sensory knowledge more acceptably rational to those in the tradition of Plato who continued to distrust sensual pleasure. And it led to what a later philosopher claimed to be "the objectification of pleasure" in the arts.* Pleasure thus was thus supposedly made into an aesthetic 'object' for occasioning personal gratification through 'works' of art and music.

As a result, the discourse of traditional aesthetics and art and music criticism increasingly rationalized the arts in accordance with Descartes's prevailing separation of the mind and body. Hence, the idea of 'appreciating' the arts became dependent on studied knowledge, intellectual analysis, dissection, and analysis of 'works' (i.e., notated scores) as "pure," autonomous, and absolute sound structures (i.e., mere stimulus objects; readers should recall their music theory and analysis classes for evidence of this). In consequence, there was a single-minded focus on strictly abstract, internal, and supposedly 'intrinsic' features and formal relations. Ever since, 'music appreciation' has been pursued educationally as a matter of *understanding* 'works' in rational, intellectual, cerebral terms—or according to certain psychological states of mind—that require study, learning, and refinement.†

Accordingly, 'music appreciation' books and courses typically consist of boiled-down surveys of music history and theory for musically untrained ('uncultivated') music lovers. The implication, of course, is that their love for music is without merit if not supported by *background knowledge* 'about' music. The program notes of concerts are a related social praxis predicated on the assumption that such information is necessary to uninformed audience members if they are to understand and thus to 'appreciate' the music about to be heard.

Yet these notes are socially central to the *business* of the 'classical' music industry.* So we always are told about the important teachers the artist studied with—an affectation that goes back to the performer who studied with . . . , who studied with . . . , all the way back to Beethoven—as evidence of an aesthetic lineage. Many pianists today are still subjected to the piano skill-drills of Czerny because of his contacts with Beethoven and his position as a teacher of Liszt.

Kant and 'Taste for Beauty'

From the very beginning of aesthetic theorizing, controversy and inconsistency reigned. The influential German philosopher Immanuel Kant at first strenuously objected to Baumgarten's theory and to the term "aesthetic." As one philosopher notes, Kant "did not approve of this use of the word 'aesthetic'. . . . [H]e used the word 'aesthetic' to refer far more generally to our sensory capacities," in other words, to aisthesis.* But, forty years after Baumgarten's *Aesthetica*, Kant's own theory of judgments of "free beauty" and the "sublime" had gradually and mistakenly been turned by aesthetic philosophers into *a theory of art*—namely that art exists to evoke "pure" aesthetic responses of the sort characterized by the concept of "free beauty."*† Unfortunately, these theorists have ignored or overlooked the fact that Kant thought art to be inferior to beauty in nature because nature is free of human impurities and *purposes*—that the problematic root of art is human *art*ifice. (In this, his philosophy was clearly wrong, since even a culture's regard for pleasures of, language about, and uses of nature are thoroughly imbued with its social categories, criteria, tastes, and sensibilities: e.g., a lake that is 'good for' swimming.)

As mentioned briefly in the Introductory chapter,† then, Kant's theory is not a theory of *art* but an analysis of his notion of "free beauty" where judgments of sense (aisthesis) can be made that are claimed to be *universal* despite being based on personal, subjective experience.† In contrast, a judgment that something is *good of its kind* is a judgment of *dependent beauty*; its 'beauty' (e.g., a flower vase or play in sports) depends on the pragmatic 'good' being served. This dependency on a personal judgment of pragmatic 'goodness' introduces a subjective variable that Kant believed detracts from universal claims, since people differ about such practical 'goods' and values.

Kant's theory of "free beauty" was developed into a theory of *'good taste for beauty'* that distinguished among "useful arts" (crafts), "agreeable arts" that merely amuse and entertain, and the 'fine arts' that are supposedly "pure" (of human biases and preferences) and thus said by later aestheticians to be beautiful "for their own sake." Thus was established (until quite recently) the lowly status of crafts (as opposed to 'fine arts') and the disdain for entertainment in connection with the 'fine arts' that has existed ever since in aesthetic discourse and 'classical' music circles. Moreover, then, in the setting off of art from life, art was argued to be somehow more 'profound' than any mere entertainment, amusement, or diversion.

Following Kant, the 'fine arts' are said to exhibit *purposiveness without purpose*. According to this criterion, the intent (purpose) of 'tasteful' (i.e., beautiful) art and music is not practical (praxial) use; the "purposiveness" in question is the sole intention of experiencing beauty, the sublime, and so on. The "sublime" was theorized in nineteenth-century Romanticism as an experience that was overwhelming. It was premised on 'wow' experiences of natural beauty such as Niagara Falls or the magnificence of Alpine vistas. Such aspects of nature lack purposiveness; they just are beautiful. Experiences of the sublime in art, however, were also said to depend on "disinterestedness"—a criterion that later aestheticians have considered to be the "aesthetic attitude" one is supposed to bring to works of art in order to properly evoke "pure" aesthetic experiences. The *disinterested aesthetic attitude* of speculative-rationalist aesthetics is thus strictly contemplative and not concerned with either practical utility or entertainment and amusement.*

This criterion is responsible, then, for the *rejection* of the idea that has existed since ancient Greece of the arts as central to daily practical life and sociality. And it is responsible for claims that 'fine art' evokes a distinctly aesthetic experiential mental state (i.e., a distinctly unique psychological essence) that is properly detached from and somehow 'transcends' ordinary experiences—a claim not supported by recent brain research of musical experience. Kant rarely mentions music and reportedly had a low regard for it. He regarded it as contaminated by its use in religion and for merely agreeable sensual pleasures. The singing of hymns by his neighbors annoyed him.

This notion of "purposiveness without purpose" and the resulting "disinterested aesthetic attitude" were amplified by subsequent aestheticians and art critics into the idea that a work of art is *autonomous* and "for its own sake" (i.e., "absolute" in and by itself, like nature), that it is separate from any ulterior or utilitarian purposes (i.e., is useless, other than being 'good for' contemplation). In effect, it is the very *lack* of such praxial (functional) conditions for 'fine art' that is supposed to promote a *properly* disinterested response. The resulting conviction is that any such praxial concerns—including entertainment values—introduce subjective preferences, interests, and needs and other practical, "dependent," or merely "agreeable" variables (Kant's terms) into what should be a pure and purifying aesthetic experience.

The social history of all such rationalist claims in the discourse of aestheticism and in the rise of the middle class (and the public concerts, discussed later) are studiously ignored by most historians, theorists, and aestheticians.† Their claims, then, for music that is supposedly autonomous of social categories and conceptual contexts of meaning are themselves, in historical fact, *social in origin*; they are (despite the millions of words expended in behalf of absolute music by aestheticians) *social inventions* (by the social system of aestheticians) that have been taken as 'true' claims about music and its values. Nevertheless, as one philosopher of music has concluded, the "autonomania" of aestheticism—the disregard of "autonomaniacs" for context, use, function, or situation—wrongly makes absolute music seem to have descended from Mars!*

Kant's theory of disinterested judgments of "free" beauty, the sublime, "aesthetic emotion,"* and so on, has thus become the shared premise of most speculative-rationalist aesthetic theories of art and music. As a result, focus is typically on an idea(l) of "pure" contemplation that is supposedly different from and 'higher' than mere sensory delight, visceral pleasures, or praxial benefits. Until the advent of praxialism, this aesthetic claim has pervaded philosophical foundations for music education at all levels.† Actually, there are other, more recent philosophies of art and music that are not aesthetics based,* which creates a further problem for those relying on aesthetic claims as a basis for music education philosophy.

The Ascendancy of Presentational Music over Participatory Musics

The rise of the institution of the public concert decidedly advanced the habit of contemplating music, as though studying animals' outward traits in a zoo and thus divorced from their natural functions of hunting, courtship, and the like. This institution obscures (see Chapter Two)† the fact that concert listening praxis is itself pragmatically 'for' the intellectual entertainment and edification of audiences (i.e., it has the purpose to fill their time rewardingly) as a worth-while spending of leisure time (Note: "Worth-while" literally means "good time," an important distinction from 'fun' time!).† Therefore, in their own way, concerts and recitals offer a unique—but, in the world of music, a quite rare—music praxis focused on audience listening. When music became a middle-class *commodity*, 'classical' music as we know it today was invented.*

With the rise of this new commodification of and commercial market for music, the number of concerts grew rapidly. Journals of art, music, and cultural criticism began to appear in large numbers. These proliferating sources also reflected the *social fashion* of aesthetic theorizing in the nineteenth century. Most of these were part of the 'grand theory' of a philosopher, thus reflecting major differences between philosophers and eras.

This spread of the aesthetic theory of absolute music diverted attention from the many praxial functions and values of music that nonetheless continued to serve daily life and leisure-time pursuits, especially of the 'uncultivated' masses.† Those in the 'cultivated' elite thus ignore the many social effects of listening at concerts. However, violations of concert etiquette—clearly social criteria—are quickly noted. (Today, of course, being seen at the symphony or opera is often a social benefit. Moreover, corporations that sponsor subscription seats to entertain their clients musically are increasingly common.).

Moreover, not accounted for by speculative-rationalist aesthetics but central to disciplines such as sociology of music, ethnomusicology, and cultural studies) are vernacular, 'popular', folk, ethnic, dance, jazz, and religious musics and, in general, musics that are not notated or that are freshly created for each new praxial occasion. The typical exclusion of these studies in the preparation of music teachers clearly seems to amount to a *refusal* by the institutional ideology of 'classical' music to acknowledge their musical merit, probably because there usually are no notated scores to study and analyze and because such musics are often readily accessible to self-taught amateurs. Perhaps such musics are a *threat* to that institutional ideology since they are far more prolific in the daily lives of most people. Musics of this kind especially include major forms of participatory musics—certainly the most prevalent kind in the world.

Participatory musics are distinguished in ethnomusicology from *presentational* musics; with the former there are no audience-performer distinctions. They exist to promote some degree or kind of musical participation by everyone (even if it is only, for example, clapping along with, moving to, or singing along with the music). With presentational musics, the performers (often professional but at least practiced, as with school ensembles) provide music for audience members who otherwise participate only as listeners.*†

However, as Alperson concluded in 1991,† a proper philosophy of music and music education needs to account for *all* music praxis—not just for the presentational concerts of music high on the aesthetic hierarchy but for the socio-musical values of the many participatory and other musics in life. This obviously includes all world music that has not been influenced by the Western philosophical notions that arose in ancient Greece (e.g., rationalism) and the speculative-rationalist aesthetics that arose following Baumgarten in eighteenth-century Europe. And it includes all musics made in behalf of ethnic, social, and 'popular' (etc.) interests and needs: no doubt the vast majority of musics in the world!

Music education, thus, has steadfastly ignored, even rejected, the preponderance of such musics in favor of music in Western presentational (mainly 'classical' traditions).† Even when participatory musics are given occasional lip service in the school curriculum—for example, the recent attention given to world and 'popular' musics—they are most often treated as presentational musics for entertaining audiences. However, when a culminating concert presentation socially shares with an audience of parents and peers the musicking of participatory praxis, the result can still be participatory—as long as the concert is not the premier premise for student participation. When participatory musics are included in the curriculum solely for concerts, they fail to properly serve as evidence or models of the sociality of music or for incorporating and encouraging lifelong participation. When school concerts are behind them, those who attended lose the participatory ethos.

Overreliance on presentational concerts presents a grave danger to the present and future health of music education.† The present world of music software and apps for computers, tablets, smartphones, and the like, for example, are all predicated on 'doing', on personal and shared praxis.† And, of course, participatory musics enjoy wide popularity around the world and contribute to the life well lived through their contributions to enhancing life.

Related Readings

Roland Barthes. *Image Music Text*. Trans. S. Heath. Fontana Press/HarperCollins, 1977; https://rosswolfe.files.wordpress.com/2015/04/roland-barthes-image-music-text.pdf (accessed June 10, 2015).
See pp. 149–150 for the epigram to this chapter and pp. 149–153 for the entire chapter. Michael Chanan (cited later) builds on Barthes' essay (27–31) as a basis for his own book, Musica Pracica.

Michael Proudfoot. "Aesthetics." In G.H.R. Parkinson, ed., *The Handbook of Western Philosophy*. New York: Macmillan, 1988; 831–856.
See p. 850 for the quotation at the beginning of this chapter and p. 852 for the later quotation about Kant's disapproval of the word "aesthetic."

David Summers. *The Judgement of Sense: Renaissance Naturalism and the Rise of Aesthetics*. Cambridge: Cambridge University Press, 1987.
*An award-winning historical account of how aisthesis (judgments of sense) **socially** evolved into aesthetic theories.*

Noël Carroll. *A Philosophy of Mass Art*. Oxford: Clarendon Press, 1998.
An important critical account of the "aesthetic theory of art," pp. 89–109.

F. A. Wright. *The Arts in Greece: Three Essays*. New York: Kennikat Press, 1969.
About music, pp. 37–73.

Howard Rachlin. "Aristotle's Scientific Method." In H. Rachlin, *Behavior and Mind: The Roots of Modern Psychology*. New York: Oxford University Press, 1994; 66–85.
Not yet science, but the beginning of empirical processes in the creation of knowledge.

Alfred Schutz. "Making Music Together." In *Collected Papers*, Vol. 2. Ed. A. Brodersen. The Hague: Martinus Nijhoff, 1971; 170–173.
Communities of musical praxis.

Peter J. Martin. *Sounds and Society: Themes in the Sociology of Music*. Manchester: Manchester University Press, 1995.
The social construction of musical meaning. A 'classic'.

Max Weber. *The Rational and Social Foundations of Music*. Trans. D. Martindale, J. Riedel, and G. Neuwirth. Carbondale: University of Southern Illinois Press, 1969.
The rational roots of Western music (e.g., scales, harmony, notation) in Western social institutions. In this account, the rational roots stem from social structures.

Zoltán Kövesces. *Metaphor and Emotion: Language, Culture, and Body in Human Feeling*. Cambridge: Cambridge University Press, 2000.
The cultural and bodily sources of emotion.

On funerals in rural China, see:
http://www.washingtonpost.com/blogs/worldviews/wp/2015/04/24/china-to-citizens-stop-hiring-strippers-for-funerals/?wpisrc=nl_wv&wpmm=1 (accessed May 15, 2015).

Jean-Marie Schaeffer. *Art of the Modern Age: Philosophy of Art from Kant to Heidegger*. Trans. S. Rendall. Princeton: Princeton University Press, 2000.
A major philosophical critique of the "spectatorship" theory of art.

Larry Shiner. *The Invention of Art*. Chicago: University of Chicago Press, 2001,
On class, taste, and market influence, pp. 75–152. An informative social history of the social "invention" of 'fine art' and 'classical' music.

Stefanie Buchenau. *The Founding of Aesthetics in the German Enlightenment: The Art of Invention and the Invention of Art*. Cambridge: Cambridge University Press, 2013.
More scholarship from cultural studies on the social invention of art and music.

David Gramit. *Cultivating Music*. Berkeley: University of California Press, 2002.
About (among other topics)˙ the power and dominance of the aesthetic ideology of music.

Tia DeNora. *Beethoven and the Construction of Genius: Musical Politics in Vienna, 1872–1803*. Cambridge: Cambridge University Press, 1995.
An important and interesting study of the rise of "serious music," "great music," and "genius" in the musical politics of Viennese Classicism as a result of the impact of aesthetic theories and the socio-musical impact of aristocratic tastes and patronage.

Anne Midgette. "How (Not) to Behave: Manners and the Classical Music Audience." *Washington Post*, April 29, 2015; http://www.washingtonpost.com/entertainment/music/how-not-to-behave-manners-and-the-classical-music-audience/2015/04/29/

111a2aa4-bc72–11e4-b274-e5209a3bc9a9_story.html?wpisrc=nl_most&wpmm=1 (accessed May 15, 2015).

Carl Dahlhaus. *The Idea of Absolute Music.* Trans. R. Lustig. Chicago: University of Chicago Press, 1991.
On absolute music as being "pure" and "sublime" in a quasi-religious way.

Carl Dahlhaus. *Esthetics of Music.* Trans. W. Austin. Cambridge: Cambridge University Press, 1990.
For the "historical starting-points" of aesthetics, pp. 1–9; for a scathing quotation from Schoenberg critical of aesthetics, p. 1.

Peter Kivy. "The Liberation of Music." In P. Kivy, *Philosophies of Arts: An Essay in Differences.* Cambridge: Cambridge University Press,1997; 179–217.
On the 'liberation' of absolute music from the real-life "veil [sic] of tears," p. 212.

Joseph E. Gould. *The Chautauqua Movement.* Albany: State University of New York Press, 1961.
A history of the educational, musical, and social influence of this important historical movement in the United States.

Theodor W. Adorno. *Essays on Music.* Trans. S. H. Gillespie. Berkeley: University of California Press, 2002.
Essays on the commodification of music and much more of social relevance by a major twentieth-century social critic.

Max Paddison. *Adorno, Modernism and Mass Culture: Essays on Critical Theory and Music.* London: Kahn & Averill, 2004.
On the commodification of music.

Theodor W. Adorno. "Bach Defended against His Devotees." In T. W. Adorno, *Prisms.* Cambridge: MIT Press, 1983; 133–146.
An interesting example of Adorno's argument that (in this case) Bach needs protection against commodification by his admirers.

Don Martindale and Johannes Riedel. "Introduction: Weber's sociology of music." In Max Weber, *The Rational and Social Foundations of Music*, trans. D. Martindale, J. Riedel, and G. Neuwirth. Carbondale: University of Southern Illinois Press, 1969; xi–lii.
A useful summary of this important sociology of music; "fine people" quotation, p. xii.

Michael Chanan. *Musica Practica: The Social Practice of Western Music from Gregorian Chant to Postmodernism.* New York: Verso, 1994.
For the quotation about positivistic musicology, see p. 38; for further details of the critique, see pp. 44, 81, 138, 165–166, 236.

Tia DeNora. *After Adorno: Rethinking Music Sociology.* Cambridge: Cambridge University Press, 2003.
On music as a dynamic medium of sociality.

Pierre Bourdieu. "The Historical Genesis of a Pure Aesthetic." In R. Johnson, ed., *The Field of Cultural Production.* New York: Columbia University Press, 2003; 254–266.
An important sociological and critical account of the "pure gaze" of aesthetics.

Pierre Bourdieu. *Distinction: A Social Critique of the Judgment of Taste.* Trans. R. Nice. Cambridge, MA: Harvard University Press, 1984.
A classic sociological critique of how "tastes" create and are created by social class and cultural categories.

Joseph Kerman. *Musicology*. London: Fontana/Collins, 1985.
On the needed change from scientific claims for musicology to a new critical (social context) orientation.

On the "new musicology" movement, see, e.g.: http://www.mtosmt.org/issues/mto. 96.2.2/mto.96.2.2.mccreless.html (accessed May 15, 2015).

Richard Kramer. *Musical Meaning: Toward a Critical History*. Berkeley: University of California Press, 2002.
A 'new musicology' perspective on "understanding music as a worldly activity" (6), not "for itself."

Kevin Korsyn. *Decentering Music: A Critique of Contemporary Musical Research*. Oxford: Oxford University Press, 2003.
A postmodern/poststructuralist critique of the "Tower of Babel" (5-10) of various 'scientific' research traditions of music.

Nicholas Cook. "Music as performance." In M. Clayton, T. Herbert, R. Middleton, eds. *The Cultural Study of Music: a Critical Introduction*. London: Routledge, 2003; 204–214.
Quotes Schoenberg on 'hearing' from the score alone (see 204) but also describes a philosophy of "music as performance" not as 'works' for performance.

Stephen Davies. "John Cage's *4'33"*: Is It Music?" In S. Davies, *Themes in the Philosophy of Music*. New York: Oxford University Press, 2003; 11–29.
The more interesting question is whether Cage would have been amused or irritated by this obfuscation.

Kay Larson. *Where the Heart Beats: John Cage, Zen Buddhism, and the Inner Life of Artists*. New York: Penguin Press, 2012.
A major study of John Cage's decidedly anti-aesthetic influence on other contemporary artists in music, dance, and visual arts.

Michael Talbot, ed. *The Musical Work: Reality or Invention?* Liverpool: Liverpool University Press, 2000.
All chapters except one criticize the 'work' concept.

Paul Crowther. *Art and Embodiment: From Aesthetics to Self-Consciousness*. Oxford: Clarendon Press, 1993.
About the role of the body ignored by aesthetics.

On Dalcroze *eurhythmics* (a praxis of the bodily bases of music), see: http://www.dalcrozeusa.org/ (accessed May 15, 2015).

Richard Shusterman. *Practicing Philosophy: Pragmatism and the Philosophical Life*. New York: Routledge, 1997.
On embodiment, somatic experience, and the arts as praxis, pp. 131–177.

Frederick C. Beiser. *Diottima's Children: German Aesthetic Rationalism from Leibniz to Lessing*. New York: Oxford University Press, 2011.
The seventeenth-century roots of speculative-rationalist aesthetics; for Baumgarten, pp. 118–155.

Antonio R. Damasio. *Descartes' Error: Emotion, Reason, and the Human Brain*. New York: Grosset/Putnam, 1994.
A critique, by a leading neurobiologist, of dualisms such as mind vs. body, reason vs. feeling, and biology vs. culture.

Lawrence W. Levine. *Highbrow/Lowbrow: The Emergence of Cultural Hierarchy in America*. Cambridge, MA: Harvard University Press, 1988.
On the aesthetic hierarchy and 'training' of audiences. An important study of the aesthetic hierarchy for culture.

Michael Talbot, ed. *The Business of Music*. Liverpool: Liverpool University Press, 2002.

Noël Carroll. *A Philosophy of Mass Art*. Oxford: Oxford University/Clarendon Press. 1998.
*Once again in this context, on mistaking Kant's theory as a **theory of art**, pp. 89–109; but also on how "mass art" (e.g., 'popular' music) violates aesthetic criteria.*

George Santayana. *The Sense of Beauty*. New York: Dover, 1896/1955.
The aesthetic theory of art as "objectification of pleasure," p. 33; on beauty as 'objectified' in 'works'.

Aaron Ridley. *The Philosophy of Music: Theme and Variations*. Edinburgh: Edinburgh University Press, 2004.
On "autonomania" and "music from Mars," pp. 1–16.

Noël Carroll. *Philosophy of Art: A Contemporary Introduction*. New York: Routledge, 1999.
A survey of nonaesthetic philosophies of art in addition to aesthetics.

Adam Krims, ed. *Music/Ideology: Resisting the Aesthetic*. Amsterdam, The Netherlands: G+B Arts International, 1998.
One of many rejecting the aesthetic ideology of art; see the cited sources.

Jacques Rancière. *Aesthetics and Its Discontents*. Trans. S. Corcoran. Cambridge: Polity Press.
A postmodern qualification of the aesthetic premise.

Stuart Sim. *Beyond Aesthetics: Confrontations with Poststructuralism and Postmodernism*. Toronto: University of Toronto Press, 1991.
Another postmodern critical study.

Patrik N. Juslin and John A. Sloboda. *Music and Emotion: Theory and Research*. New York: Oxford University Press, 2001.
A survey of theories (often conflicting) of "musical emotion."

John Sloboda. *Exploring the Musical Mind: Cognition, Emotion, Ability, Function*. Oxford: Oxford University Press, 2005.
See the sections on emotion (pp. 175–296), and also on talent (pp. 275–316).

Malcolm Budd. "Emotion." In D. Cooper, ed., *A Companion to Aesthetics*. Oxford: Blackwell, 1993; 134–138.
A summary on "aesthetic emotion"; see in the same volume the entry on "aesthetic pleasure," by Jerrold Levinson, pp. 330–335.

Thomas Turino. *Music as Social Life: The Politics of Participation*. Chicago: University of Chicago Press, 2008.
Participatory vs. presentational musics (and studio composed/arranged musics). An important study from ethnomusicology.

2

OBSCURUM PER OBSCURIUS

It would be hard to think of a subject more neurotically self-doubting than aesthetics. Claims that the subject is dreary, irrelevant, muddled and misunderstood have been a persistent theme, not only of recent, that is to say, post-war [World War II], writers, but from the very start of the subject. Alas, these claims have all too frequently been justified.

Michael Proudfoot*

This chapter explores the philosophical fallacy of *obscurum per obscurius*: the attempt to *explain something that is already obscure in even more unclear terms*, thus making it even more difficult to understand. Recourse to aesthetic premises and terminology for music education fails heavily on this account. Music is simply more vital, more important, more valued, and in more and more ways, than aestheticians can describe. Their writings may fuel their academic careers, but—as already mentioned—nothing of their theorizing can affect or improve how an individual actually responds to a musical praxis. Audiences don't study aesthetics; nor do teachers or their students!

. . .

Aesthetic This and That

The rationalist (though not always rational) speculations of various aesthetic theories engage in just such obscuring of music's very obvious and powerful affective appeal. Consider young children, for example, who decidedly do not contemplate it aesthetically and who yet enjoy it immensely (thus, evidence against the aesthetic theory of art and music and small "p" theories of 'music appreciation'). Aesthetic rationales are simply not needed in order to account for the *moving power* of music and art. The powerful attraction for what one leading and outspoken critic of aesthetics (and an artist herself) calls our "latching on" to music and art, the way a baby latches on to the nipple.* This analogy as to how the arts provide life sustenance is very fitting.

39

Music may well be the most deeply *felt* of all the arts. Trying to explain that power by recourse to the rationale of "aesthetic emotion" can be compared to trying to account in intellectual terms for the evident appeal of certain foods or the charms of nature. As the noted contemporary visual artist Barnett Newman complained, "aesthetics is to me like ornithology must be to birds." Thus, leading figures in the arts today reject and rebel against eighteenth-century aesthetic theory with its quaint notions of why art is important and how it is to be received. For all but academic aestheticians, it appears that the aesthetics of music died a quiet death early in the twentieth century when faced by the avant-garde and proliferating 'isms' guiding music away from eighteenth-century aesthetic fashions.

In what still persists, the various aesthetic theories of art hold that a certain quality called beauty (or the sublime,† expression, or, "aesthetic emotion"†), depending on differences between aestheticians and philosophical trends, somehow results from the "aesthetic properties" of musical 'works' in a way that is in some sense absolute and universal and that transcends time and place. From the onset, however, aestheticians in this tradition have disagreed as to whether such properties are *objectively* (formally) 'in' aesthetic objects ('works' of art) or whether they only occasion a *subjective* response 'in' an individual. With the "disinterested aesthetic attitude"† detaching or separating music from daily and personal life contexts, 'works' became the focus of interest and the carriers of value (not their social benefits for audiences and other social attributes).

The center of attention for leisure time contemplation and intellectual study is then focused on this autonomous detachment of music from life.† These 'works' are thus regarded as the source of the supposedly timeless and thus impersonal intellectual value attributed to the canon of Great Works mentioned in the Introduction.† Social scholarship, especially "listening history" that analyzes the important variables that influence changes in situated listening habits and experiences over history, is usually dismissed by orthodox musicology.* For example, consider the changing social variables of concert house architecture* (over history; or, today, in-the-round vs. proscenium stages), changing social variables (concert attire and programming), audience conduct (when to clap or not), performance practices (concerto performers who no longer improvise the cadenzas), improvements in instrument manufacture (from the seventeenth to the twentieth century, often in response to ever-larger concert halls; e.g., the piano), effects of recordings on listening praxis (the effect of having heard a composition many times via recordings), socioeconomic status (seating placement in a concert hall or having to listen only to recordings), and the fact that recordings involve the musical results of important decisions made by recording engineers, and so on. These and other social influences and variables are thus dismissed or ignored in the education of most musicians, including music teachers.

Furthermore, consider the claims of the *authentic music movement*.* It attempts to recreate a performance of a 'work' (from a historically 'authentic' score) as it is believed to have been heard by the listeners of its day (or sup-posedly intended by the composer: what some aestheticians call "the inten-tional fallacy")* by using period instruments and scholarly research. It mostly ignores important social variables that influenced "the music" as it was pre-sumed to have been heard in earlier times. But, for example, not considered is the proposed 'authentic' Bach score as heard in the discomforts a dark, cold, and damp Baroque church that involved the semiotics—symbolic aspects—of space (i.e., in contrast to a modern concert hall) and that assuredly influenced the ability of instruments to stay in tune. Claims to authenticity also accept the implausibility that the music of Bach, for example, could be heard with a seventeenth- or eighteenth-century sensibility by twenty-first-century listeners who have already experienced Beethoven and Brahms, or Brubeck and the Beatles or James Brown, Anthony Braxton, or Pierre Boulez.†

Also overlooked are the questions of who were the members of audiences of any time in past history (members of the royal court, intelligentsia, bourgeoi-sie, working class?) and why they were listening (e.g., for social, ceremonial, religious, or secular interests?). These important social variables influence "the music" that is heard. A performance in the splendor of a king's palace, attended by members of the royal court, noblemen and women, and other notables and dignitaries certainly brought a vast array of social values to the listening expe-rience that are entirely missing today. For example, consider the early con-cert custom that had the king and queen seated in full view of the audience so that the audience could respond as much to the responses of the royalty as to the music—maybe even more. Yet such social variables give way to a single-minded preoccupation with the 'works' studied by music historians and theorists.

Any personal involvement or personalizing of response that is 'for' the Self, such as the enjoyment of music for personal pleasures, emotional catharsis, or mere affective delight (especially the visceral response often mentioned by listeners: "The music sent chills up my spine")* is regarded as aesthetically unsuitable and unseemly by the aesthetic theory of art. Because music is held to be autonomous† and 'in' the mind, not the body,† and "for-its-own-sake,"† attention is directed to the internal relations or "expressive properties" of the 'work' rather than with any "extra-musical" conditions external to it or that support its performance or use. This is the dogmatic gospel of "absolute" music mentioned in the previous chapter.†

Thus, the connection of music with praxis (i.e., in terms of music's social purposes and values)—for example, with music as worship, celebration, cer-emony, and so forth—either disqualifies it as properly aesthetic or consid-erably lowers its value on the tacit aesthetic hierarchy,† depending on the theorist. Religious music moved to the concert hall becomes "aestheticized" and secularized (e.g., Handel's *Messiah* or Verdi's *Requiem Mass*) much as religious art removed from situated praxis to museums becomes *an*esthetized as 'fine art' (e.g., a carved Baroque altar removed from its Baroque church for viewing in a secular art museum devoid of the rest of the symbolic meanings in a church). The result of such a focus on Great Works is what one music philosopher calls "the imaginary museum of musical works."* Praxis or anything else "extra-musical"—for example, for aestheticians who extol absolute music (i.e., the words of vocal music† and the titles of "program music")—is held to contaminate music's 'for-itself' purity.*

Autonomania

This separation of art from the practical, personal, and social is a unique consequence of the aestheticized philosophy of art and music found in Western culture. In other cultures (e.g., those in Asia, Africa, and elsewhere), in stark contrast, art and music regularly serve everyday life and are valued in terms of their praxial use, not their rarity.

"Everyday aesthetics"* is a new philosophy of art that critiques and goes beyond speculative-rationalist aesthetic theories. The mention of "aesthetics" as "everyday" would be a contradiction if not for the fact that the term "aesthetics" is understood by this philosophy in praxial terms to mean maximizing the benefits of aisthesis or artistic sensibility in everyday life— to living a life of everyday beauty. Such saturation of everyday life by art and music (and crafts and many other sources of sensibility) is also valued by the pragmatic tradition of John Dewey's *Art as Experience.* Dewey recommended that daily life be lived with heightened aisthesic awareness and lived artfully.† Such newer philosophies of art are slowly beginning to overcome the undue domination of the speculative-rationalist ideology and the dogma of absolute music. But so far music education has taken little notice.

The very situated everyday and special circumstances in and for which music is actually created or appreciated that are so steadfastly denied, ignored, or rejected by speculative-rationalist aesthetic philosophy are, however, *very* relevant to music understood in its original role as praxis.† When these contexts and circumstances are ignored, the philosophical muddle that results and the overall falseness of aesthetic theory to the actual experiencing of the pleasures of art and music lead many contemporary analytic philosophers to *doubt* the philosophical legitimacy of speculative-rationalist aesthetics (e.g., the epigrams for Chapters One and Two). Aesthetics therefore has a legitimation crisis† of its own among analytic philosophers.

Among the many reasons, then, for aesthetics being regarded by many analytic philosophers as the "stepchild of philosophy"* are the ambiguity of its terminology and the inconsistency of its logic. Despite, then, the ample use of aesthetic qualifiers (aesthetic this, aesthetic that, aesthetic whatever you want to label as aesthetic), aestheticians typically fail to distinguish (a) "aesthetic experience" (ontologically: about whether it exists) from other kinds of experience or from *musical* experience; or (b) "aesthetic properties" (epistemologically; as sources of knowledge) from nonaesthetic properties or from *musical* features; or (c) "aesthetic emotions" from general or everyday emotions;† or (d) "aesthetic values" from *musical* or *praxial* values.

As the philosopher Ludwig Wittgenstein concluded, the ability to respond to art and music does not rely on learning or using aesthetic terms and concepts (as is obvious with the responses of children to music: pay attention to those!). At most, he noted, adjectives such as "beautiful" are interjections that substitute for facial expressions and other gestures of subjective approval. In fact, aside from making noble-sounding aesthetic claims about music, *musicians rarely use aesthetic terms* in their praxis; they use musical terminology or ordinary language.*

Terminological imprecision is therefore all too typical in aesthetic discourse—especially aesthetic rationales for music education. Widely different, even conflicting, theories are often marshaled in what is a misguided attempt to make music and thus music education appear noble and profound. For example, leading theories of aesthetic education often draw on both Kant and Dewey, even though Dewey was opposed to the tradition of the aesthetic theory of art that has stemmed from Kant.*

Thus, the diverse ways by which different aestheticians attempt to define or otherwise account for aesthetic experience typically run afoul of the philosophical *fallacy of equivocation*. As a result, the meaning of "aesthetic" this and that constantly varies, either according to the context or the aesthetician or, in centuries past, according to the part art and music (as expected at the time: another social variable) played in a philosopher's ''system' (e.g., Schopenhauer, Hegel, and many others, all typically at odds with other).† Thus, irresolvable arguments between speculative aestheticians exist about whether aesthetic "meaning" is timeless and pure or situated in relation to context, history, and individuals.

Disagreement is also widespread about whether music engages morality or politics or is steadfastly neutral (generic; from Mars†) or somehow transcends any "extra-musical" contaminations. *Monists* argue that aesthetic meaning and value are intrinsic to 'works' and thus unchanging. *Pluralists* argue, instead, that aesthetic meaning is always diverse and ever-changing. Monist views ignore the diversity, situatedness, and the ever-evolving sociocultural nature of human interests, emotions, and needs, while *aesthetic pluralism* can extend to the radical subjectivism of "beauty is in the mind of the beholder."

Most music lovers, among them some music teachers, typically regard such speculative-rationalistic aesthetic theorizing as endlessly circular and thus as irrelevant to how, when, where, and why they experience and value music. Like most musicians, they rarely think or speak using the discourse of aesthetics that, for the most part, is unknown to them since it is not included in their education. This would seem to be a considerable liability if, as aestheticians claim, music is inextricably ruled by aesthetics and thus demands mastery of many esoteric terms and concepts! For example, readers of Part One of this book who "don't care" about such distinctions only prove the point: *obscurum per obscurius*.

They should care, however, because, in their curriculum documents, advocacy statements, and pedagogy, music educators often rely on an (explicit or tacit) aesthetic *rationale*, rather than a warranted *philosophy*, for the value and relevance of music education based on exactly aesthetic speculations and theories.† Again: Their basic assumption is that simply engaging in musical "experiences" and "activities"—whether in classroom music or ensembles—is "aesthetic" and that it *automatically* promotes and improves students' aesthetic responsiveness and, presumably, their 'good taste' and improved dispositions for 'good music'.* This assumption is dysfunctional, and the resulting *legitimation crisis*† (see Chapter Three) is empirical evidence of a major source of a lack of community and administrative support for music education in schools. While the aesthetic theory of music lacks consequences for 'real-life' musicking, it surely has had negative consequences for the health of school music!

The Sacralization of Music

The aesthetic rationale—despite teachers' lack of understanding of aesthetics—is often offered in teachers' rationales and advocacy for school music, perhaps because aesthetic values sound nobly like other important, righteous, profound or solemn religious, ethical, and intellectual values. Historians of Eurocentric culture have thus noted what they call the "sacralization" or "sacred calling" of artists and musicians whereby, over history, art and music have taken on a quasi-religious role.* Some scholars have even concluded that the transcendental, almost mystical, spiritual nature accorded to aesthetic experience has replaced the religious dimension of life that was pushed aside in Western history by the Enlightenment's championing of reason and science. As one leading contemporary aesthetician, Peter Kivy, states (in good conscience), "art has taken on something like the place of religion in our lives" and thus is accorded something of an otherworldly status.*

With art having thus become quasi-religious, then, aesthetics has served as its 'theology'. But just as many people can be quite uninformed about the theological particulars of their religions (e.g., small "r" religious belief?), music educators (and most musicians and audience members) are similarly uninformed about aesthetics. And the problem is that the more one knows about musical aesthetics, the less relevant the discipline seems to be to what actually happens in the various worlds of music. Christopher Small, music sociologist, educator, and musician, coined the term "musicking" (sometimes also spelled "musicing") to convert "music" from a noun—a 'thing'—into an action—a 'doing' or praxis.† The term thus goes back to times in history when "musick" (as it was spelled then) was praxial. When asked to review a history of aesthetics (by Lippman, cited in the related readings), he found that "most of it bore very little relation to anything I recognized in my own musical experience, as listener, or as performer, or as composer."* Perhaps readers have the same impression from the present survey of aesthetics.

The field of aesthetic theorizing thus seems to have advanced scholarly careers more than it has enlightened why—and the ways in which—ordinary people actually engage with music in enhancing their everyday lives. And that makes aesthetics a weak and unproductive foundation for advocating the inclusion of music education in schools.† Most members of the school and social community (including music teachers) obviously know little or nothing about aesthetics, but they do like music!

The typical view of schools held by members of the public, politicians, and administrators (whose decisions are typically political) thus takes what sociologists of education call a *functionalist* position. The public expects schools to serve various practical functions of importance to society: political, economic, social, and personal. Actually, functionalist theories have been widely opposed in recent scholarship by newer sociological theories (e.g., interpretative, critical, and conflict theories). However, functionalism is the 'common sense' view held by voters and politicians. And it leads schools to be battlegrounds between different groups in society as to whether schooling effectively meets the functional needs of society, whether what is needed is being taught and learned, and the like.

From a functionalist perspective (and from the competing sociological theories predicated on different premises),* it seems fair to conclude that school music is losing ground in the competition for scheduling and resources because the idealistic and religious-sounding assertions of "aesthetic education" are so vague and the results so intangible. The value of their *function* in life is not at all clear or convincing to students, administrators, or the public. In any case, a serious challenge facing school music advocates is that, in their own educational careers, most taxpayers and school authorities themselves have apparently failed to experience the aesthetic values claimed by music educators!†

Instead of having recourse to such quasi-religious speculation, we need only to properly acknowledge the immense *aisthesic* drawing power music has for everyone, regardless of age, socioeconomic standing, demographics, or education. By simply accepting the powerful attraction of music as a natural, human given, the various psycho-cultural-biological-cognitive-sources and down-to-earth praxial premises for music education can promote pragmatic results on the part of more people and the various modes of musicking in which they engage. This outcome would be to the benefit of music and music education.

Beliefs that *music* education is a species of *aesthetic* education, in contrast, have clearly not fulfilled their premises or promises to students and taxpayers—no doubt because of systematic weaknesses in the speculative-rationalist rationale offered by aesthetics in attempting to account for our musical pleasures. And, not surprisingly, if the philosophical grounds and practical premises are weak, the results can only be weak—even nonexistent or negative. If, in fact, students have been either 'turned off' to or 'untouched' (in the most 'feelingful' sense of that word) by the aesthetic rationale of school music, a major problem exists.† Similarly, because music is everywhere in life, it seems useful and pragmatic to seek and explore other, more pragmatic premises for offering music as part of the general education of *all* children—for a general education that can serve them throughout life, including musically. Since the public is interested in *functional* benefits, a pragmatic praxial view offers the best chances for success in convincing local communities that, in fact, "music is basic" in schooling.

What Is the Value of School Music?

What is needed, then, is clarity concerning the aims and benefits of school music stated in unambiguous, functional (i.e., praxial) terms, not the vague, unverifiable premises or promises of aesthetic dogma. Under praxial conditions, the *tangible* results of music education become so obvious that reasonable people, even in difficult economic times, cannot doubt the contribution of their music education in schools to their daily lives.† Such clarity would dispel the "it's nice if you can afford it" attitude, the belief that music education is but a frill compared to academic studies. And the claim that "music *is* basic" would be recognized as a *social fact*, not just an advertising slogan.†

We need not obscure what is perfectly obvious: Music of all kinds is an absolutely central feature of contemporary life. Moreover, given the rapid growth of various music media, it is going to continue to be central to the life well lived. We don't need aesthetic speculations about music's values; those values for people are right before our eyes and ears every day. Look around and listen. The overwhelming presence of music in today's society demands a philosophy of music that is responsive to contemporary needs, not a dubious relic from the rationalistic speculations of the seventeenth to the nineteenth century.

Related Readings

Katya Mandoki. *Everyday Aesthetics: Prosaics, the Play of Culture and Social Identities*. Burlington, VT: Ashgate, 2007.
A major critique, by an artist, of aesthetic premises for art, and a defense of the alternative concept of "latching on," pp. xvi–73.

Charles Rosen. "Beethoven's Triumph" (essay-review of J.H. Johnson, *Listening in Paris: A Cultural History* [Berkeley: University of California Press]), in the *New York Review of Books* 42(14) (September 1995): 52–56.
A rejection of "listening history" by one of the world's leading musicologists. Would you agree after reading the next citation?

James H. Johnson. *Listening in Paris: A Cultural History*. Berkeley: University of California Press, 1996.
A "listening history" of how listening praxis has changed over the ages and why.

Paul Throm. "Authentic Performance Practice." In T. Gracyk and A. Kania, eds., *The Routledge Companion to Philosophy and Music*. New York: Routledge, 2004.

Colin Lyas. "Intention" and "Intentional Fallacy." In David Cooper, *A Companion to Aesthetics*. Oxford: Blackwell, 1995; 227–232.
Key concepts often ignored by small "p" philosophy.

Donald A. Hodges and David C. Sebald. *Music in the Human Experience: An Introduction to Music Psychology*. New York: Routledge, 2011.
Research about common "physical responses to music," such as "chills," pp. 184–186.

Lydia Goehr. *The Imaginary Museum of Musical Works*. Oxford: Clarendon Press, 1992.
"The" seminal critique by a music philosopher of the 'works' concept of music.

Yuriko Saito. *Everyday Aesthetics*. New York: Oxford University Press, 2007.
No focus at all on the aesthetic ideology, just on enhanced living through aisthesis.

Crispin Sartwell. *The Art of Living: Aesthetics of the Ordinary in World Spiritual Traditions*. Albany: State University of New York Press.
The "everyday aesthetics" (aisthesis) of non-Western traditions and their lessons for us.

Michael Proudfoot. "Aesthetics." In G.H.R. Parkinson, ed., *The Handbook of Western Philosophy*. New York: Macmillan, 1988; 831–856.
A critique of aesthetics as the stepchild of philosophy; why many analytic philosophers discredit aesthetics. See p. 831 for the quotation at the beginning of this chapter.

Ludwig Wittgenstein. *Wittgenstein Lectures and Conversations on Aesthetics, Psychology, and Religious Belief*. Berkeley: University of California Press, no date.
A pragmatist-oriented philosophy by a major philosopher who holds that "meaning" is a function of use, pp. 1–40.

Lawrence W. Levine. *Highbrow/Lowbrow: The Emergence of Cultural Hierarchy in America*. Cambridge, MA: Harvard University Press, 1988.
On the sacralization of music, pp. 85–168.

Pentii Määttänen. "Reimer on Musical Meaning." *Action Criticism, and Theory for Music Education* 2(1) (September 2003); http://act.maydaygroup;org/articles/Maat tanen2_1.pdf (accessed May 15, 2015).
A critique of, among other problems, Bennett Reimer's contradictory reliance on both Kant and Dewey to rationalize aesthetic ideology.

Bennett Reimer. "Music Education as Aesthetic Education: Past and Present." *Music Educators Journal* 75(6) (February 1989): 22–28.
By the main advocate of aesthetic theory of music for music education.

Bennett Reimer. "Music Education as Aesthetic Education: Toward the Future." *Music Educators Journal* 75(7) (March 1989): 26–32.
Part II of the preceding article.

Bennett Reimer. *A Philosophy of Music Education: Advancing the Vision*, 3rd ed. Upper Saddle River, NJ: Pearson, 2003.
The "vision" in question is following the aesthetic ideology. This text has been criticized for confusing philosophy with an advocacy rationale.

Bennett Reimer. "The Experience of Profundity in Music." In L. Bartel and D. Elliott, eds., *Critical Reflections on Music Education: Proceedings of the Second International Symposium on the Philosophy of Music Education.* Toronto: Canadian Music Education Research Center, 1994; 101–126.
An aesthetic rationale.

K. B. DeMarrais and M. D. LeCompte. *The Way Schools Work: A Sociological Analysis of Education,* 3rd ed. New York: Longman, 1998.
About functionalism and other sociological theories of education: conflict theory, Critical Theory, and more.

Thomas A. Regelski. "Praxialism and 'Aesthetic This, Aesthetic That, Aesthetic Whatever'." *Action, Criticism, and Theory for Music Education* 10(2): 61–99; http://act.maydaygroup.org/articles/Regelski10_2.pdf (accessed May 15, 2015).
A detailed critique of aesthetic premises for music education.

Edward Lippman. *A History of Western Musical Aesthetics.* Lincoln: University of Nebraska Press, 1992.
A history of aesthetic theories (plural).

Peter Kivy, ed. *The Blackwell Guide to Aesthetics.* Oxford: Blackwell, 2004.
On music as a quasi-religion, pp. 11, 325–339.

Larry Shiner. *The Invention of Art: A Cultural History.* Chicago: University of Chicago Press, 2001.
Art as having become a redemptive and a quasi-sacred calling, pp. 187–212.

Christopher Small. "Musicking: A Ritual in Social Space." In R. Rideout, ed., *On the Sociology of Music Education.* Norman: University of Oklahoma School of Music, 1997; 1–13.
A brief account of musicking as a verb form.

Christopher Small. *Musicking: The Meanings of Performing and Listening.* Hanover, NH: Wesleyan University Press, 1998.
An important scholarly account of musicking as a verb form and of the many social facets of performing and listening; should be required reading for teacher candidates.

3

PREDICTABLE PROBLEMS OF AESTHETIC THEORY AS A BASIS FOR MUSIC EDUCATION

*A critical-thinking educator of any kind works to develop a personal and professional disposition to question carefully both old and new ideas, to balance thinking and feeling, to question authority, to participate in critical and ethical dialogues with others, to construct thoughtful viewpoints, to think imaginatively, to make judgments that are fair and rational, and to apply the results of his or her critical thinking in actions that are congruent with personal beliefs and desired outcomes. . . . Critical **reflection** takes critical thinking one step further. In critical reflection, we assess why and how our **past** thoughts, feelings, and actions have led to our current ways of thinking and doing.*

David J. Elliot and Marissa Silverman*

Having surveyed the failure of aesthetics to account reasonably for people's love of music, we now detail the predictable practical difficulties that such assumptions bring about for the daily praxis of teaching music. It examines the conditions that lead music education, as pursued on the aesthetic rationale, to all kinds of everyday problems for teachers. Some of these concerns involve predictable issues with students. Other concerns deal with various kinds and degrees of failure to effectively educate students musically. In addition to resulting in the loss of students who drop out (actually or mentally), these failures lead to the mounting need for advocacy in support of school music that has resulted from the speculative aesthetic claims made for the benefits of music education.

Music teachers too often dutifully repeat taken-for-granted advocacy claims rooted in the aesthetic theory of music. As former school students, however, they might benefit from critical reflection that might well reveal the futility and dangers of such claims. For example, were those classmates in ensembles who didn't go on to major in music "aesthetically" educated in important and lasting ways? As adults, are their tastes much different from or noticeably better than those of students who were not in ensembles? And how much of a contribution to musical life after graduation were general music classes rooted in the 'music appreciation' assumptions of aesthetic theory?† What follows offers perspectives on these and other important questions and issues.

. . .

Aesthetic Metaphysics as Premises for Music Education

Many teachers will be familiar with student resistance to aesthetic premises for music. Teachers of what is called "general music" (i.e., classroom music) are especially vulnerable to students' resistance and protestations (typically manifested as misbehavior) when faced with teaching that follows the aesthetic education premises of 'music appreciation'. However, ensemble teachers may be less aware of the problems created by their taken-for-granted premise of providing an "aesthetic education." They can and sometimes do achieve high musical standards. Nonetheless, one criticism of school ensembles from the perspective of the aesthetic ideology for education is that, because of the youth of their members, student groups cannot attain the excellence and artistry of professional performance, and thus their efforts fall short and give a false impression of full aesthetic values (whatever those are said to be).

A further problem, of course, has to do with the question of what exactly is advanced educationally by such activities. What is the 'good' served by years in an ensemble if the students don't continue with the musicking into their adult lives? The answer typically given (and that was a focus of the critique of Chapters One and Two)† is that concert performances of a (limited) selection of programmed compositions over the years have inevitably amounted to aesthetic experience and therefore are automatically a worthwhile and productive educational endeavor.† However, at least from the aesthetic perspective, much of the literature performed by school ensembles is not of the 'highest' musical quality as far as its musical complexity is concerned, and it thus fails to elicit the 'high' aesthetic values connected with the professional concert literature. In fact, much of the professional concert literature has no parallel in the music performed by school ensembles: No choirs singing spirituals, no concert bands playing anything (with an exception for touring military bands and those at universities), and few of the Great Works of orchestral literature are possible. Attempts to interest and attract students by programming arrangements of popular music, film music, light classics, and the like are, of course, quite typical and are thus susceptible to this aesthetic objection.

In a praxial perspective, however, there is no such aesthetic hierarchy. There is only an endless source of musics of value and interest. But, from a praxial perspective, performing such presentational musics in concerts is not an end in itself. Thus, in contrast to the premise that just performing is automatically aesthetically valuable, a praxial approach to teaching is concerned instead with developing *independent musicianship* and the *dispositions* for continuing in a variety of presentational and participatory formats† outside school and after graduation.

In terms of curriculum,† beliefs based on aesthetic premises are usually unstated (i.e., are tacitly held)† and are highly idiosyncratic and often differ

50

between teachers. And, as noted already, most musicians and music teachers are not extensively informed about aesthetics, the philosophy of music (which involves more than just aesthetic theories), or various social and cultural studies of music that stress music's many social roles and dimensions. Therefore, it can be easy for teachers to uncritically repeat taken-for-granted assumptions about the "aesthetics of music" as definitive. As a result, their reflex is to adopt aesthetics-based *sloganeering* as part of their advocacy for music education in schools. Consequently, given the variability, imprecision, and speculations of aesthetic theory and the sacralization of music and art described earlier,† faith in aesthetic theorizing by music teachers is held with almost reverent regard.

This religious-like faith in aesthetic metaphysics, however, is not a properly stable *philosophical* or functionally *pragmatic* basis for music education in schools. As has been seen, music teachers thus sometimes try to articulate in everyday language a variety of vague and taken-for-granted aesthetic assumptions, for example, that "music is organized sound" or that "music is the language of the emotions" or that "music expresses the composer's inner life."† However, such small "p" philosophical claims are simply uninformed about the many very contentious issues at stake in the philosophy of art (e.g., formalist vs. expressionist theories, the institutional vs. the aesthetic theory of art, the "intentional fallacy," art as representation).* Thus, as regards aesthetic theories of music, such assumptions are not coherent in any sense an aesthetician might accept or understand. Furthermore, such notions among music teachers, even in the same school system, are frequently different, even at odds.

In any case, such beliefs can be incongruent with a teacher's actual teaching habits. Or the results of that instruction can be dysfunctional or nonpragmatic in ways that contradict their aesthetic claims. For example, pedagogies featuring heavy doses of skill-drill using uninteresting or unmusical materials often seem to turn off more students than are led to the predicted heights of aesthetic enlightenment.† Whether in private studios or rehearsal halls, such methods (didactics) too often fall short of the noble aesthetic benefits claimed. Their *an*esthetic (i.e., benumbing) traits routinely discourage and thus reduce participation by, in effect, functioning to 'sort out' those unwilling or unable to submit to the demands of the aesthetic creed and its few devoted student acolytes. However, such dedicated students often simply join the school activity for the *sociality of musicking together*, altogether unconcerned with aesthetic criteria. This motivation is especially typical for adolescents for whom sociality of any kind is paramount. (This also accounts for disruptive socializing during rehearsals.)

The 'weeding out' of the unworthy—and attending selectively to only the brightest 'flowers'—is, unfortunately, too often typical of music education in many of its models at all levels. It is also a major *ethical failure* to provide and promote a productive music education for *all* students.† Thus, serious inequalities often exist in providing a useful music education to those many students who, for whatever reason, do *not* gravitate to school-based presentational ensembles or who prefer various kinds of participatory musics not typically accounted for or valued by the aesthetic theory of art and thus not often included in school curriculums. The claimed superiority of the 'good music' taught in school can therefore result in pushing aside and distancing itself from all the musics outside the school that are otherwise important to people of all ages.

The Disinterested Aesthetic Attitude

In particular, the "disinterested aesthetic attitude"† that is said to be a criterion for aesthetic experience is obviously difficult to teach, inspire, or encourage in the formal school curriculum. Students may be disinterested in or bored by some their academic studies. But they are decidedly not disinterested or bored regarding the role of 'their' music for their lives! For young children, furthermore, music is clearly a species of *play* that is not ever 'strictly musical' or 'for-itself' in the "disinterested" way aestheticians contend. (Keep in mind that we *play* music and that the verb is crucial; when the play impulse is lost and musicking becomes *work*, students look elsewhere for ways to spend their time in worth-while ways.)†

Furthermore, such "aesthetic disinterestedness" (i.e., the "aesthetic attitude")† is also contrary to the developmental trajectory young children and even less relevant to nine- to twelve-year-old students in the upper elementary years and to adolescents in middle and high school. Students of these ages* typically approach music most enthusiastically in terms of various forms of praxis—that is, according to a wide range of highly social and personal *functions*, not the least of which is the *personal identity** that comes from membership in cohorts that social psychologists of music call musical "taste groups."* In this regard they are not much different from adults who identify with 'classy' music. If the purpose of music education is to *convert* (in almost the religious sense) students' various music preoccupations and inclinations to 'for-itself' musical autonomy along the lines speculated on by aesthetic theories and rationales, then the claim certainly has failed to be convincing to policymakers, school leaders, and taxpayers! Where this is the case, the failure is evidenced by the constantly growing need for advocacy in light of mounting challenges to the very existence of school-based music education.†

Intangibility of Aesthetic Improvement

Moreover, the *covert* (nonobservable) nature claimed for aesthetic responding—that is, an *inner* state of mind—is an altogether unworkable premise for guiding teaching! Without *observable results* as clear evidence of teaching and learning success, there is simply *no indisputable way* of empirically observing whether the hypothesized 'aesthetic responsiveness' of students is in fact being educated, advanced, expanded, or improved. Thus, there is no sure way of assessing whether teaching and learning have been effective! There is, as a result, no accountability for results—by students or teachers.

What is worse, on the taken-for-granted assumption that all musical experiences are aesthetic, teachers too easily conclude that simply promoting musical "activities" and "experiences" in the classroom, rehearsal, and concert hall is automatically and inevitably aesthetically educative and valuable. The result is that their teaching is uncritically rationalized as contributing to a student's aesthetic responsiveness simply on the basis of various kinds of mere *exposure* to music. However, such "experiences" and "activities" too often do not contribute in practical, useful ways to a student's musicianship or musical independence or to the dispositions or attitudes that incline students, as adults, to enhance their lives along the lines of the musical diet offered by school music.†

Efforts to translate speculative-rationalist aesthetic theories into practicable and pragmatic lessons and rehearsals are thus too often habitually content instead with a host of unsubstantiated (philosophical and pedagogical) speculations about 'music appreciation' understood as aesthetically contemplating music. As we have seen, a common philosophical (small "p") speculation is that preliminary study (i.e., background information *about* music) is needed to perceive, understand, and respond to the formal relations and expressive and other "aesthetic properties" of autonomous works. Thus, the claim is that without this cognitive and cerebral foundation, any 'appreciation' is superficial. You can't just love music; you are supposed to know the *why* and *what* of responding to music properly.†

A second speculation concerns performance lessons and ensembles: that the experience of performing automatically promotes the relevant musicianship for properly understanding and appreciating music as an *audience listener* and thereby automatically encourages 'good taste' throughout life. First of all, any benefits of this claim depend on the director or teacher. Director-teachers who make all musical decisions for students simply do not promote the independent musicianship needed to "transfer" (as educational psychology calls it) from performing to audience listening praxis. But even where teachers advantageously involve students in musical decision making (i.e., explain reasons for musical decisions made and promote the students' knowledge of criteria for musical judgments), the listening needed for performing in an ensemble—listening with a laser-beam focus on one's part—is often very different from holistic audience listening—which is more like a floodlight.*

And in judging the musical choices of most students and school graduates (i.e., the public), there is simply no substantial evidence that students subjected to such aesthetics-premised instruction in their school years have been predictably enabled or inclined as adults (a) to be contemplative connoisseurs of the 'classics'; or (b) to participate as adults in performing 'good music' as serious amateurs; or (c) to exhibit 'taste' dispositions any different from or better than that of those who have lacked such instruction. In fact, the lack of notable evidence that aesthetics-premised education has produced *musical* progress of enduring value itself points to what many aesthetes are the first to bemoan as a crisis in Western culture (or Culture): the oft-heard complaint that the prevailing musical tastes of young and adults alike are overwhelmingly oriented to various 'popular' and vernacular musics instead of to the 'good music' that is high on the aesthetic hierarchy.

These complaints by aesthetes are themselves evidence of the lack of any fundamental pragmatic contribution of the aesthetic rationale of music education to the tastes and lifelong musical choices of most school graduates—or, for that matter, to the out-of-school musical choices and tastes of student musicians. Such advocacy made on behalf of assertions for music's aesthetic virtues therefore makes empty claims that cannot be backed up by tangible results that demonstrate a lasting, pragmatic difference in the lives of students while students and as graduates.† It should come as no surprise, then, that orchestras and opera companies are under siege almost everywhere, with declining and greying audiences. Thus, when music education is conducted according to the aesthetic ideology, it too often falls, so to speak, on *deaf ears.**

Legitimation and Advocacy

Endlessly debated aesthetic theories and taken-for-granted aesthetic assumptions, then, are simply unable to serve music education in tangibly useful or unifying ways. The vagueness of the terminological "aesthetic this and that"; the extreme variability and unresolvable contradictions between different aesthetic theories; the intangibility of claims made; and the public's lack of understanding of or support for such insubstantial and otherworldly claims—all these have led to a major *legitimation crisis* for music education premised on the aesthetic ideology.

A legitimation crisis arises when inherent contradictions or intrinsic flaws in the *functional* purposes a social institution claims to serve regularly fail to produce those actual functional benefits.† Consequently, the institution gradually loses social support for continued existence in its present form. Take, for example, in music history, the "piano duels" where pianist-composers competed against each other in the art of improvisation: Mozart vanquished Clementi, and Beethoven, of course, defeated his rivals. This peculiar institution no longer exists, perhaps because of the demise of interest in it or of the skills needed. (So, no longer do virtuosi improvise their cadenzas; all is 'scripted' to their greater glory.) In modern terms, the community bands that were popular in the 1940s and 1950s in the United States have thus largely disappeared in favor of garage bands and music apps. In the case of school music, at stake is the institutional rationale based on aesthetic claims for music education: the *promise* that school music promotes increased aesthetic edification and the enrichment of musical taste.

Thus, in school-based music education, teachers, at least in much of the Western world, constantly have to defend or advocate (i.e., propagandize) for the value of musical instruction as an important part of the *general education of all students*,† rather than for only the select (or selected) few disciples willing to study and submit to music study as a rigorous discipline. These are usually in large presentational ensembles that serve only a small percentage of all school students (especially the highly selective ones). The resulting challenges to the institution's continued existence thus necessitate repeated attempts at *legitimation*.

In music education, these rationalizations typically take the form of advocacy claims that politically advertise values and benefits of school music that in fact have not been noted or appreciated by society. In effect, then, verbal attempts to 'sell' music education to the public, taxpayers, and school officials on the basis of an aesthetic rationale of musical value are needed to defend against the abundant evidence that such advocacy of aesthetic premises for school music has been no more successful than the aesthetic benefits promised. Such advocacy usually tries to explain away any need for change and describes and defends the status quo as in fact good or good enough.

The failure of the aesthetic rationale to "sell" school music to taxpayers often seems to be recognized by many music teachers themselves. Rather than concern themselves with improving the *musical results* of their teaching, they instead turn to the rationale that studying music has social benefits, such as increased personal discipline and responsibility. Of course, such focus and self-control are benefits of all school studies, not a benefit of schooling that can be credited to music study alone. Another oft-made contention is that studying music improves general intelligence, that it makes students "smarter." This so-called "Mozart Effect" has no scientific basis.* It demonstrates only how reckless advocacy that ignores the many social benefits and enjoyments that are natural with musicking can be.

Paradoxically, advocacy often has the effect of discrediting opponents—in our case, the public, taxpayers, and school administrators—as misinformed or ignorant about the aesthetic importance of school music, *thus blaming the victims*!† Ironically, then, in effect it criticizes the very people who should have benefited from and thus who should support school music programs. Or it promotes the original aesthetic rationale in new, improved-sounding versions. In such challenges, only minor, often inconsequential changes are made. (The study of social institutions shows that most seek to defend their continued existence as unchanged as possible; science is an exception.) Thus, rather than significantly rethinking basic premises and paradigms in terms of contemporary concerns, challenges, and circumstances (e.g., world musics, music apps, proliferating 'crossover' musics, and participatory musics), advocates or followers of the aesthetic rationale seek instead to defend and hence *preserve* the status quo with only minor changes. In public forums advocates mistakenly assume that just mentioning "aesthetic this and that" makes an effective impression. Judging by the crisis facing school music educators, this advocacy is not working!†

Yet, many accept and defend the traditional and ideological status quo of school music education, despite the social challenges to it, rather than accept the problems and weakness of their aesthetic and other assumptions. This book is intended, in part, to earnestly consider the evidence and the reasons *why* school music has been challenged in recent years. The time is ripe, then, to reconsider the usual premises that musical activities and experience are automatically 'good' and aesthetic. Instead, it is time to accept a new (but old) model for musicking: the ample social and empirical evidence that music as social praxis is more pedagogically pragmatic and much more likely to attract public attention.

Music Education as a Conserving Activity

More than a casual relationship exists concerning the values of music education between "conservative" and "conservatory" philosophies. As a university president once noted to me, "Changing a music faculty is like moving a cemetery." Education—including music education—*is*, of course, properly a conserving activity focused on preserving and transmitting the past. But, in addition to this *transmission* function identified by the sociology of education as promoting social stability and continuity,† schooling also needs to bring the past to bear in relevant ways on the present and to effectively lead to the future. *Transformation* theories of schooling, then, focus on the need for social change and progress, for example, on eliminating social inequality.*

Music education based on aesthetic rationales, however, often promotes *inequality*—at least musical inequality—by favoring its uncritical assumptions (small "p") about 'good music' and 'talented students'. The social result, thus, is *not* serving (at all, or adequately) the musical needs, interests, and lives of those many students who (for whatever reason) are neither interested in nor suited to meaningful participation in the typical diet of presentational school music ensembles: band, chorus, and orchestra. This is unfair and unjust* for an institution that exists on the premise of contributing to the benefits of music in the general education of all students in school.†

As a result, too many students fail to have their *legitimate* musical interests and needs met by school music—interests often inspired by the many models of musicking outside the schoolhouse doors but not offered (or offered enough) in school music curriculums. This lapse represents a serious *ethical* failing.† Moreover, the tangible and lasting value of their musical education for the few served by presentational school music ensembles also remains elusive. Most give up their school-based musical involvement upon graduation, and their musical choices and tastes as adults give no evidence that they are *musically* different from those graduates who were not in presentational school ensembles.

One major challenge in recent years to the aesthetic ideology has been the criticism by multicultural and world music proponents* that the "music" of music education has problematically been limited mainly to the presentational Western 'classics'—or 'classics-like' arrangements, as is frequently the case with much of the school ensemble literature.* Institutional acknowledgment (too often in lip service more than in fact) of musics other than Western 'classics', however, has not stopped institutional mindguards from making aesthetic claims for such inherently praxial musics. Their reasoning agrees with the aesthetic ideology that collects "primitive art" in museums as though it were created for aesthetic contemplation rather than for use (e.g., decorated war shields, useful objects, religious artifacts).* And with the occasional exception of jazz (or recent and fleeting 'pop' favorites), the participatory (and often ethnic) musics that are abundant in many communities are usually not centrally included in the musics of music education programs. Thus, school music curriculums† fail to draw upon or contribute to the musical vitality of the community. This again results in the need for ever more advocacy.

Music Education versus the Aesthetic Ideology

The dominant institutional model for music education—in a computer analogy, its *default setting*—has clearly been and continues to be the acceptance by most music teachers of the aesthetic ideology. To it alone can be attributed the many challenges to the methods and legitimacy of music education that have music educators in the Western world constantly on the defensive. Nonetheless, they are all too willing to accept or utter—and are even sometimes dogmatically committed to accepting or uttering—fine-sounding aesthetic rationales in their teaching, curriculum documents, and advocacy pronouncements.

Even so, despite their belief in "aesthetic this and that," they cannot propose clearly defined overt outcomes—beyond the next concert or next rote song in general music classes—as either the basis of curricular or daily planning or for evaluating instruction and learning in terms of future benefits. Indeed, most music educators—like the conservatory musicians who trained them—simply take the assumed aesthetic value of music for granted—and thus ignore its perfectly evident social roles. They personally enjoy making music with their students. But their students too often end up serving the teacher's musical interests and needs—strong musical dispositions instilled in musician-teachers by their own teacher education programs. After four years of such intense (but limited) musicking, they often cannot imagine the praxial alternatives for school music students who are *not* interested in musical careers. In fact, even the most musically advanced students are often not interested in such careers. Their interest, we hope, is in the benefits of musicking, not in taking a first step on the way to a musical profession.

Teachers thus cannot calculate instruction on aesthetic grounds; they simply cannot devise lessons that clearly and demonstrably advance the frequency or depth of the claimed aesthetic experience. Thus, advocacy claims that school music amounts to an aesthetic education often amount to not much more than empty clichés. Were those music teachers not so enchanted by the vagueness of aesthetic posturing into which they have been socialized by their university studies, it would be obvious to them, as it is to those outside the school-based institution of music education, that most school graduates give little or no evidence that such teaching has amounted to an effective *music* education. Far too often, the musical studies of most students seem not to have 'made a difference' in their *musical* lives.*

Graduates of classroom music in Western societies (i.e., "general music" in the United States), then, typically have acquired few musical skills and little knowledge they can or are disposed to use outside class and after classes are completed! The scheduling of such required classes (in behest of educational policies that give 'lip service' to the arts but don't support them economically) is being cut back in many schools; in others, class sizes have grown to unwieldy numbers. Students who have 'had' such required classes (in the United States, often grades K–8, though more and often less generously) act as though they are *immune* to having to take any more (like a disease "I 'had' that now I'm immune to and won't have it again"). Thus, they steadfastly avoid such electives—assuming that high school general music electives are even offered, which is less and less likely given the lack of student interest and the increasing problems of teaching staff reduction! Furthermore, those who have had private lessons and have been in school ensembles also give little or no evidence of either a willingness or an ability to employ their limited skills, developed from a narrow range of presentational concert literature, when the years of school music are over—or, too often, even when the school day is over.

Moreover, as ensemble membership becomes more and more demanding of dedication and ever more selective from elementary through middle to high school ensembles because of the musical criteria inherited by teachers from their university days, the percentage of students choosing to take part typically drops disturbingly. This gives rise to the criticism from taxpayers and others that the programs are *elitist*, serving only a motivated few.† And worse: As a result of such declining numbers, the teaching staff is often reduced. One school that started 175 band students in grade 5 (nine- to ten-years-old) had only 35 left in the high school band, and thus a second band position was eliminated!

School music has thus unfortunately become its own extremely limited and limiting musical praxis that comes with what seems to be a do-not-use-beyond-the-school-years (or school-day) *'shelf-life'*. It may serve the socializing, 'need-to-be-good-at-something' motivation, the recognition* and extracurricular *social* needs of a small percentage of students while they are in school more than it develops any functional breadth and musical independence that predictably serves *all* students in their musical futures. In sum, aesthetic premises are so logically and pragmatically problematic that they are simply not suitable to either the legitimation or the practical challenges of teaching music in schools effectively.

The Bottom Line

Music education in schools would not be so involved with its legitimation crisis to begin with if the benefits of the social institution were readily notable to the public (i.e., pragmatic) in their effects and thus seen by students, parents, and taxpayers as valuable in terms of lasting benefits for out-of-school and after-graduation music praxis. The concept of *immanent critique* in Critical Theory takes the claims made by an institution for the benefits of its existence as empirical criteria for assessing the institution's promises. Claims of aesthetic education fall far short of this criterion and also fall short of an effective *music* education. Thus, and sadly, many graduates will admit: "I love music, but I don't know anything about it"; or ". . . , but I have no talent for it"; or ". . . , but I can't carry a tune."

Such attitudes have been *learned* from—actually *taught* (although inadvertently)—as a part of the "hidden curriculum"* *by* music teachers. Because aesthetic theory has not been part of teachers' explicit training, the aesthetic assumptions unwittingly at stake in their teaching are usually 'hidden' from them as well. However, the implications of such tacitly held small "p" philosophies† are usually acutely sensed by students and graduates. They especially note the unspoken curricular *disapproval* that fails to include 'their' (or other) musics—the musicking they do or encounter outside school—as a valued part of the school curriculum.† Given their impressions, only "approved" musics are included, though often the criteria for approval are left unsaid and the grounds for disapproval of other musics equally go unmentioned but sensed.

(This problem of "approved" versus "unapproved" musics implied by curriculum inclusions/exclusions does not usually arise in most other school subjects. Students are then problematically more aware of their musical lives—and music in society—than they are of the social implications of their studies of history, science, or many other subjects. Perhaps they should be more aware: for example, studies of racism, social inequality, sexism, religious themes, and the like. But these are often excluded or stifled on grounds of not disturbing the comfortable social status quo. If music were studied critically, according to studies of racial, ethnic, and nationalistic social criteria, the social status quo would be far less accepted!)

The opposite small "p" philosophy—that school music should cater entirely to the present musical preferences of students—is equally limited and limiting. What point is achieved by promoting what students already accept as musically interesting? Just as language arts teachers seek to extend language skills beyond the 140 characters of Twitter (and actual words, spelling, and grammar), so music educators can expand the advantages of music in its many forms: everything from jazz, rap, and rock to new 'classical' musics that have long ago bypassed aesthetic theories of 'good music'. Music today is so rich in its forms that "new musics" of various kinds can 'cross over' from any aesthetic claims and appeal to students' modern sensibilities (aisthesis). So, the fact that students are already musicking outside school—at least listening to their 'popular' preferences—does not mean that other musicking interest cannot be inspired, expanded, and advanced by school music.† And, finally, the fact that the typical *means* and purposes of musicking are essentially praxial doesn't mean that the *ends* produced are not profoundly meaningful.

. . .

Fortunately, the praxial theory to which we can now turn in Part Two *is* relevant and practical because it is rooted in life and articulated in the terms of pragmatic philosophy and social theory. Since it is grounded in philosophical naturalism (with its focus on observable events, not otherworldliness) and action theory (not on transcendental, quasi-religious, speculative-rationalist aesthetic claims), it advances basic *musical* skills and general musicianship that competent teacher-musicians can easily translate it into successful praxis.

Related Readings

David J. Elliott and Marissa Silverman. *Music Matters: A Philosophy of Music Education,* 2nd ed. New York: Oxford University Press, 2015.
  For the quotation at the beginning of this chapter, see p. 10.

Noël Carroll. *Philosophy of Art: A Contemporary Introduction.* New York: Routledge, 1999.
  An introduction to philosophies of art that are not all based on aesthetics.

Martin Stokes, ed. *Ethnicity, Identity and Music: The Musical Construction of Place.* Oxford: Berg, 1997.
  The importance of music for ethnicity and identity; note especially in relation to adolescents developing identity in school music programs.

Thomas A. Regelski. *Teaching General Music: A Musicianship Approach.* Oxford: Oxford University Press, 2004.
  On the developmental traits of pre- and early adolescents (ages 9–12), see pp. 29–51 as regards music education (general music or instrumental).

Philip A. Russell. "Musical Tastes and Society." In D. J. Hargreaves and A. C. North, eds., *The Social Psychology of Music.* New York: Oxford University Press, 1997; 141–160.
  Beyond "taste," the entire book offers much of relevance for an understanding of musical sociality.

Kevin Shorner-Johnson. "Building Evidence for Music Education Advocacy." *Music Educators Journal* 99(4) (June 2013): 51–56.
  The 'evidence' might better be empirical data of the benefits of music education, not the usual futile rationales.

David M. Hedgecoth and Sarah H. Fischer. "What History Is Teaching Us: 100 Years of Advocacy." *Music Educators Journal* 100(4) (June 2014): 54–58.
  If we still need advocacy after a hundred years, what are we doing wrong?

Thomas A. Regelski. "Accounting for All Praxis: An Essay Critique of David Elliott's [1994] *Music Matters." Bulletin of the Council for Research in Music Education* 144: 61–88.

For Elliott's reply, see the Praxial Music Education website: http://www.nyu.edu/ education/music/musicmat (accessed May 15, 2015).

John Rawls. *Justice as Fairness: A Restatement*. Cambridge, MA: Belknap Press, 2001.
Perhaps 'the' most influential statement on social justice.

Richard A. Peterson and Roger M. Kern. "Changing Highbrow Taste: From Snob to Omnivore." *American Sociological Review* 61 (October 1996): 900–907.
Interesting research on the expansion of highbrow musical tastes—probably even more so in the past twenty years.

Dolf Zillmann and Su-lin Gan. "Musical Taste in Adolescence." In D. J. Hargreaves and A. C. North, eds., *The Social Psychology of Music*. New York: Oxford University Press, 1997; 161–187.
A sociology of musical "taste."

Lucy Green. *Music on Deaf Ears: Musical Meaning, Ideology and Education*, 2nd ed. London: Institute of Education, University of London, 2008.
Addresses the common problem of teaching that 'turns off' students to school music.

On the "Mozart Effect" see: John Sloboda. *Exploring the Musical Mind: Cognition, Emotion, Ability, Function*. New York: Oxford University Press, 2005; 379–380, 396–402.
For a summary of findings of recent research at Harvard, see: https://www.youtube. com/watch?v=oqSY3INIxAs (accessed May 15, 2015).

Minette Mans. *Living in Musical Worlds*. New York: Springer, 2009.
A study of world musics.

Sally Price. *Primitive Art in Civilized Places*. Chicago: University of Chicago Press, 1991.
A study of the problem of removing 'objects' from their sociocultural contexts for 'classy' museum purposes as 'art'. Compare to aesthetic claims made for indigenous musics.

Thomas A. Regelski. "Music and Music Education—Theory and Praxis for 'Making a Difference'." *Educational Philosophy and Theory* 37(1) (January 2005): 7–27. Issue republished as *Music Education for the New Millennium: Theory and Practice Futures for Music Teaching and Learning*. Oxford: Blackwell, 2005; same pagination.
An exposition of a pragmatic criterion for music education.

For the "need for achievement" (nAch) in motivation theory, see: Andrew M. Colman, *Oxford Dictionary of Psychology*, 2nd ed. New York: Oxford University Press, 2006; 494.
The 'drive' (nAch) to be 'good at' something and for social recognition for meeting high standards is common among school music students. It often doesn't last, however, once they find out other realms to be 'good at'.

K. B. DeMarrais and M. D. LeCompte. *The Way Schools Work: A Sociological Analysis of Education*, 3rd ed. New York: Longman, 1998.
On transmission vs. transformation, pp. 5–40; on the hidden curriculum, pp. 13–14, 242–247.

Part Two

THEORY INTO PRAXIS AND PRAXIS INFORMED BY THEORY

4

"PRACTICE THEORY" AND PRAXIS

Understandings . . . are carried in social practices and expressed in the doings and sayings that compose practices. In particular, what something is understood to be in a given practice is expressed by those of the practice's doings and sayings that are directed toward it. Meaning, consequentially, is carried by and established in social practices. Practices, furthermore, embody organizations, which circumscribe the meanings and arrangements set up and otherwise encompassed in them.

Theodore Schatzki*

As introduced in Part One, the aesthetic ideology of music is severely compromised by social theory of all kinds. In particular, the concept of music as social praxis is supported by *practice theory* in sociology, social theory and social philosophy, cultural studies, and curriculum theory. From the perspective of practice theory, music is not only 'good for' moments of leisure or rare or special occasions. Concerts, recitals, and at-home (or MP3 listening) represent only one (though an important) kind of musical praxis.

More broadly speaking, musicking, in all its forms, is a key source of *social harmony* that creates and reinforces vital social meanings and cultural realities. Like language (another central social praxis), music is shaped by at the same time that it is a building block shaping society, and it is an important source of *social* and *personal agency.* Agency, in either sense, is defined as action undertaken to bring about certain desired results (i.e., praxis), and it involves the goal of change for the better. Music as a source of agency also is creative of Self, of personal identity, and of social relationships.* It takes a dedicated ideological denial of music as inherently social to premise music as "autonomous" and to neglect the all too evident social dimensions and benefits of musicking for the 'good life'.

. . .

"Practice Theory" and Praxialism

The premise of *music as social praxis* does not rely on speculative-rationalist aesthetic theories of music and musical value; it challenges them!† Such theories, as seen in Part One, simply hypothesize various supposedly metaphysical, transcendental, and universal values for music. Or they describe musical meaning in analytic, intellectual terms and thus ignore or reject music's very evident praxial value and affective appeal for individuals and society. A praxial philosophy freely acknowledges that music has many easily recognized, affectively moving attractions that are well suited to its various social roles: from concert listening, to dancing, to the endless list of personal and social functions that give rise to different musics and their related practices and to which music is always central, not a mere accompaniment (e.g., music chosen for a wedding). Such praxialism thus advances a clearly pragmatic alternative to speculative-rationalistic aesthetics as a basis for a philosophy of music education.

From a praxial perspective and in decided contrast to aesthetic speculations, musical meaning and value are seen empirically in the wide-ranging *choices* by which individuals and society engage with musics of various kinds on a regular basis.† Thus, the *meaning* of music is what people actually choose to *do* with it and how, why, and how often. The scholarly discipline concerned with the "cultural study of music"* thus goes well beyond the study of notes in relation to other notes, or aesthetic speculations. Instead, it studies *musical meaning* in terms of music's central role in creating and facilitating "culture"—including but not at all limited to 'high culture'. In this sense, "culture" is the interacting network of multiple forms of social praxis, and is a primary source of meaning in our lives.* Musical culture, then, involves the many means by which music is meaningful in people's lives.

Importantly, then, what qualifies as musical praxis expands beyond performing, composing, and audience listening (the most central pursuits). Musicking involves any and all actions involving music, such as the collection of recordings, music criticism, the selected use of music for all kinds of physical exercise (e.g., aerobics, jogging), the creation and recording of playlists, and the sharing of playlists on social media, as well as music apps, music therapy, mood music, music in advertising and business, and all the many common uses for music in daily life.† Music, then, is clearly an opportunity for "good time" (not just fun), the valued spending of time. (Recall that "worth-while" literally means "good time").

Understood praxially, music is 'good' not only for special times and places (i.e., not only for presentational recitals and concerts—though those are important forms of musical praxis!). It fills dull moments, enlivens others, and creates sociocultural events that centrally depend on it. This is perfectly evident when noting, for example, the increasing popularity of music apps for various kinds of media, ranging from 'musicky' games (e.g., GuitarHero®), to composition software, to MIDI performance options, to recording party mixes, to the creation of sound tracks for homemade videos and much more. The world of music is far more extensive for most people than just concerts. (A self-appraisal by the reader should reveal the personal importance of music outside of concerts—or the dictates of the curricula of schools of music).

Music is called into existence by and therefore serves both to meet special social needs (e.g., rites and rituals, celebrations and ceremonies) and as an important sociopersonal resource by which everyday life is constituted—in part, certainly, but always as an important part. Accordingly, music is not 'for-itself' as the aesthetic ideology insists. Instead, and importantly, it is an important source of *interactional synchrony*—the creation, preservation, and transformation of social and cultural solidarity by which individual brains are linked or coordinated via shared socio-musical experiences.†

Beyond the obvious fact, then, that music is "performed," *music is performative*. As understood by the philosophy of language, certain "performative statements" create realities that didn't previously exist: for example, "Let the meeting begin" (creates a meeting) and "I thee wed" (creates a marriage). And words can affect and even change a present reality: "Leave me alone!"

So, too, music has an important *performative* sociocultural role. It creates social events and realities, such as concerts, dances, or participatory musicking; it also imbues social occasions with its exceptional ability for "making special" otherwise humdrum or routine occasions.* In this important perspective from cultural anthropology, music and the arts—all musics, not just those 'high' on the aesthetic hierarchy!—are *natural* human capacities that serve the equally natural human trait of sociability. Thus, the arts are not a creation or mere 'expression' of an already existing cultural mind-set or presence. Society and culture are themselves creations of the innate human impulse to mark certain human interactions and events as having special social meaning and value.

As introduced earlier, even recorded music enjoyed in private is saturated with this social synchrony.† The sources of sound and how and why they are produced and organized are all conditioned by a host of social factors that range from geography (e.g., governing the materials available for making music instruments; sea shells not brass wind instruments), to the shaping forces on music of the social institutions to which it is central (e.g., music in the format of the Catholic mass, the *shaku hachi* flute music of Zen, the trance inducement of drumming traditions, and the social commentary of rap, 'pop', and country musics). The dynamics of the recording industry, of course, are also permeated with social dimensions and subtleties. The stars of the 'popular' music industry in particular socialize—and are keenly followed—on social media sites. So are 'classical' composers (though less so, according to social fashion).*

Hence, all music is a historical *result* of and at the same time *contributes* to the social cohesion that binds individuals into societies, cultures, subcultures, and nations. It is a distinct and important form of human ordering and societal organizing. It decidedly is *not* a matter of "pure" patterns of sound that are presumed to be enjoyed for their own sake. Thus, its meanings and values are always situated in the various socio-musical cultural traditions, contexts, communities of practice, and institutions that bring it into being (e.g., ceremonies, rites of passage, celebrations, concerts) and that it always serves.*

Accordingly, music's value is not its *rarity* or purity. Very much to the contrary; its value is seen in its very evident and *abundant* sociocultural meanings and contributions. Therefore, its value is not its *in*accessibility to all but a 'cultivated' few; it is seen in the many forms by which music praxis is readily accessible to all people (and would be more so were school music to advance such options). Music, in this sense, is as pervasive as language. And it is as a central to culture as is the spoken word. Perhaps it is more central in key ways for creating the musical bonds that are so important to cultural meanings.

Appreciation as Use; Music Teaching as Promoting Use

Consequently, as introduced in Part One, consideration of musical meaning or value apart from music's various *contexts* and *communities of use* is futile and misleading.† The concept of 'music appreciation' is thus properly seen in use: *People use or put into musical praxis what they appreciate musically*, and they value such musical praxis accordingly.† They further commit themselves to the meaningful contributions a particular form of musicking directly makes to their lives. What is *not* appreciated in this sense by people is regarded by them as irrelevant (i.e., as personally useless). Thus, it is not made a regular part of their lives.

As a result, the musics people regularly choose to enliven and invigorate their lives *are appreciated in exactly the ways and to the degree they are used*—whether that is listening to recordings of hymns, attendance at concerts (of various kinds of music), participatory (and community) musicking, amateur performance, or engaging in a wide range of music-related interests (collecting CDs, sharing compositions on social media sites, using apps, and so on). A personal history of *appreciation* of these kinds promotes *future participation*. Moreover, whatever is participated in and is thus preserved in a cultural community constitutes a valued musical practice.*

Consequently, *the central ways in which musics are used in society are the proper bases of music education curriculum*. More precisely, the creation in schools of communities ("cohorts") of musical interest and learning is the goal: for example, a bell choir, a composition club. Through incorporation in schools and private studios, various key forms of musical praxis should be promoted in ways that enable and encourage them to be used throughout life and that enable them to be shared as part of communities of musical knowledge and meaning. Such praxis serves, then, as a philosophical and sociological basis for curriculum. In Sweden, the criterion of "from life into school" guides curriculum theory, thereby ensuring that schooling is relevant to students and society.† (As is explained in Chapter Seven in connection with Action Learning and "breaking 100 in music," the praxis-based curriculum theory advanced here adds "and back into life." Accordingly, students are encouraged to bring their music education into their daily lives and thus musically transform themselves and society.)†

68

Teaching for 'appreciation', then, is teaching that *through use* seeks to *promote use*. It is teaching that improves the *likelihood* of use and the pragmatic *skills* and *independent musicianship* that can encourage music's contribution to the life well lived through music. It is teaching that develops a *disposition* for musicking of some meaningful kind in life. It does not 'turn off' learners by recourse to uninspiring facts and "background information." (As has been quipped, "If we taught sex education the way we do 'music appreciation', no teenager would have anything to do with sex!")

As we have repeatedly seen, then, traditional aesthetic notions of 'music appreciation' routinely depend on teaching dry music theory and historical information 'about' music. The speculation involved is that in order to contemplate music cerebrally or 'properly' (i.e., the way trained musicians do, as though their training were the only or best way), it must be *understood* in terms of "background information" and concepts.† This criterion for appreciation is very rarely observed in most other arenas of life, for example, the foods or films we appreciate. More usually, once a kind of music is appreciated in and through praxis (i.e., experience), it leads to further interest, to study, and to the benefits of *praxial knowledge*—accumulated practical knowledge that serves future musical experience.†

Consequently, a praxis-based curriculum† is predicated instead on incorporating actual, real-life musical pursuits that are widespread and easily available and accessible in society (at least regionally or locally). Focus is on common types of musicking that help constitute the praxis of everyday personal and social life and that thus constitute culture as an interlocking network of such practices. Such teaching is not 'about' music or "for its own sake"; it is an education *in*, *of*, and *through* music.

This involves a major distinction in learning theory between "knowing how to" and "knowing that or about."† The knowledge 'of' music gained by praxis-based teaching therefore has an intimate and personal sense. It is 'from' (and 'for') musicking and its attendant values, as experienced in practical and always social terms. It requires actually involving students in musicking of various kinds and promoting their progressive ability and disposition to be active with one or more musical practice.

The benefits of being involved in several forms of musicking are facilitated by developing *general musicianship* (and vice versa). Such a range of musical skills and understandings are common to more than one kind of music. For example, basic knowledge of chords, fingerings, instrumental techniques, note reading, playing by ear, and the like can apply to several musics. With such general skills, then, the same student may take part in a bell choir and in steel pan drumming. *Praxis-specific musicianship*, in comparison, involves knowledge and skills that apply mainly to one kind of music, for example, the improvisation, blue notes, and 'swinging' groove of jazz or techniques for harmonica.

Making a Pragmatic Difference

When *what* is taught does not (or cannot) transfer to life outside or after graduation from school to active and lifelong musicking of some degree and kind, then its inclusion in a curriculum should be doubted. Without what educational psychologists call "transfer of learning"†—in this case from school into life—students will not have acquired a *functional appreciation* of the relevance, usefulness, and meaningfulness of such teaching for their future musicking. Their musical studies will have not made a notable pragmatic difference in their lives*—thus creating the earlier mentioned legitimation crisis† that motivates the increasing need for advocacy rationales.

Whatever students learned that didn't "transfer" was short-term—usually because it was conveyed in abstract or "merely academic" ways that have little or no capacity to 'move' or motivate them outside school and later in life toward an important role for music in the life well lived. Or, because it was not regularly used in pursuit of meaningful praxis, it is forgotten or discarded. Again, such musical learning has failed to 'touch' students, in the most 'feelingful', intimate, and consequential sense of that term. As a result, any musicking they may do in later life is often not a direct result of their school music experiences.

In contrast, praxial theory is supported by the philosophy of pragmatism, especially as articulated by John Dewey. Praxially, Dewey's notion of "art as experience,"† noted earlier, is understood as *life lived artfully,* intensely—in the present moment (e.g., "stop to smell the flowers," set an attractive dinner table), through enhancing the range and quality of each student's capacities with and dispositions for one or more musical praxis. The pragmatism of C. S. Pierce (who is widely credited with 'inventing' pragmatism) is focused on the role of *habits* of practice and their use.*

However, the possibility always exists that what was given focus by inclusion in a curriculum *is* appropriately relevant to lifelong musicking but that *how* it is taught fails to regularly bring about pragmatic benefits. A praxis-based music education, however, minimizes this negative outcome because it is *musical praxis* itself that is the *content* of teaching (not aesthetic this and that or academic "background information"). This requires (a) that music teachers be competent in the musicianship and other relevant criteria (e.g., interpersonal, technical requirements) of the musicking in which they engage their students; (b) that they take pedagogical steps to ensure that formal musical learning can be applied *independently* by students and graduates in the everyday conditions of musicking in society; and (c) that they employ appropriate and effective evaluative criteria regarding musical quality and progress.

In this, again, the kind of praxial music education argued for in the chapters that follow has an extremely down-to-earth, pragmatic focus in promoting the importance of music to the life well lived and that enriches a community's shared musical life. For such praxialism, the failure of students to prosper and flourish musically cannot be explained away or ignored. *Learning problems* of students (especially the kind or degree that can lead to giving up, loss of motivation, not practicing) require redoubling teaching efforts. Such problems are symptoms of the teacher's need for conscientious and careful reconsideration of pedagogy and materials studied (even of the type of musics studied)—not as evidence of a student's lack of 'talent'. In particular, such problems experienced by students are acknowledged and responded to by the teacher as an important part of *critically reflective* professional praxis.*†

The failures of the medical professions worsen or even die. The failures of music teaching simply quit lessons or ensembles, 'tune out' during general music classes, or remain unaffected by prescriptive 'delivery-lessons', lessons predicated on 'music appreciation' and related aesthetic values. Such students will have little to do with music in their present or future lives that can be credited to school music. Therein lies the challenge—ethical and practical—to music educators. How can the many obvious benefits of musicking in personal life and society become the basis for a curriculum that is based on those benefits, not on claims about "aesthetic this and that" or that music makes students smarter?

A beginning step in answering this question is to forsake reliance on the aesthetic ideology and pseudo-science and to focus instead on the tangible ways in which music resides in the lives of diverse music lovers. That provides an empirical basis for 'music appreciation'.

Related Readings

Theodore R. Schatzki. *The Site of the Social: A Philosophical Account of the Constitution of Social Life and Change.* University Park: University of Pennsylvania Press, 2002.
For the quotation beginning this chapter, see p. 58. The rest of the book details "practice theory" and the institutions that, building on sociality, are the sources of social life and meaning.

Tia DeNora. *Music in Everyday Life.* Cambridge: Cambridge University Press, 2000.
A compellingly interesting sociological study of music's role in people's lives.

Roger L. Taylor. *Art, an Enemy of the People.* Atlantic Highlands NJ: Humanities Press, 1978.
Against the aesthetic ideology as class based and dysfunctional.

Martin Clayton, Trevor Herbert, and Richard Middleton, eds. *The Cultural Study of Music: A Critical Introduction.* London: Routledge, 2003.
An important collection of articles about the cultural roots of musical "meaning."

Ellen Dissanayake. *What Is Art For?* Seattle: University of Washington Press. 1990.
A significant study from cultural anthropology of the evolutionary (natural) bases of art and music.

Ellen Dissanayake. *Homo Aestheticus: Where Art Comes from and Why.* New York: Free Press/Macmillan, 1992.

Especially see Chapter Four on "making special": the natural human tendency to mark, via art and music, certain sociocultural practices as special.

Dina Kirnarskaya. *The Natural Musician: On Abilities, Giftedness and Talent.* Trans. M. H. Teeter. New York: Oxford University Press, 2009.
Psychological study of the 'natural' and universal ability for music; despite the title, not in support of inherited 'talent'.

'Classical' musicians on the Internet and social media:
For example, a new media site created about John Cage by Michael Tilson Thomas: www.nws.edu/JohnCage/. And how about cellist superstar Yo-Yo Ma's Facebook page, with 424,217 "likes"!

Zygmunt Bauman. *Culture as Praxis.* London: SAGE, 1999.
Culture as the intersection of a network of social praxis; by a leading social theorist.

Etienne Wenger. *Communities of Practice.* Cambridge: Cambridge University Press, 1999.
A social account of meaning, learning, and identity via communities and their social practices. In decided contrast to a Piagetian focus on the individual learner, this book has a Vygotskian orientation to learning as a member of a community (e.g., classes, in schools).

Richard J. Bernstein. *Praxis and Action: Contemporary Philosophies of Human Activity.* Philadelphia: University of Pennsylvania Press, 1971.
A very useful survey of philosophies of praxis and action theory.

Hans Joas. "A Sociological Transformation of the Philosophy of Praxis: Anthony Gidden's Theory of Structuration." In H. Joas, *Pragmatism and Social Theory.* Chicago: University of Chicago Press, 1993; Chapter Seven.
Other chapters on pragmatism and social theory are also useful.

Thomas A. Regelski. "Music Appreciation as Praxis," *Music Education Research* 8(2) (July 2006): 281–310.
'Music appreciation' as use.

Thomas A. Regelski. "Music and Music Education—Theory and Praxis for 'Making a difference'." *Educational Philosophy and Theory* 37(1) (January 2005): 7–27. Issue republished as *Music Education for the New Millennium: Theory and Practice Futures for Music Teaching and Learning.* Oxford: Blackwell, 2005; same pagination.
In support of a pragmatic criterion for 'music appreciation' as praxis.

John Dewey. *Art as Experience.* New York: G. P. Putnam's Sons/Perigee, 1934/1980.
A classic exposition of a pragmatic philosophy of art in opposition to orthodox neo-Kantian aesthetics.

J. Scott Goble. *What's So Important about Music Education?* New York: Routledge, 2011.
A philosophy of musical learning based on the pragmatism of Charles Sanders Peirce.

Donald W. Schön. *The Reflective Practitioner.* New York: Basic Books, 1984.
'The' seminal study of critically effective professional praxis.

Stephen D. Brookfield. *Becoming a Critically Reflective Teacher.* New York: Jossey-Bass/Wiley, 1995.

On "what it means to be a critically reflective teacher," pp. 1–29; the rest deals with how.

Thomas A. Regelski. "Action Learning: Curriculum and Instruction as and for Praxis." In Marie McCarthy, ed., *Music Education as Praxis*. College Park: University of Maryland Press, 1999; 97–120.

A praxial view of music curriculum. See other content of interest in the collection.

Thomas A. Regelski. "Ethical Dimensions of School-Based Music Education." In W. Bowman and A. L. Frega, eds., *The Oxford Handbook of Philosophy in Music Education*. New York: Oxford University Press, 2012; 284–304.

An examination of Aristotle's ethics in relation to music teaching as praxis.

5

PRAXIS AS AN ALTERNATIVE TO AESTHETIC THEORY

*The noun **praxis** . . . is used in a broad sense to refer to any intentional action . . . and in a narrower one to what results from deliberation . . . and deliberate choice. . . . As the virtue of excellence of the calculative part of the soul [mind], practical-wisdom's unconditional end is thus **eupraxia** or excellent **praxis** of the deliberately chosen sort.*
C.D.C. Reeve (on Aristotle's term)*

We can now turn to a more detailed account of what the concept of praxis entails as an alternative both to the aesthetic theory of art and to the status quo of music education. This account begins with another acknowledgment of the *aisthesis* that is the source of the "making special" and powerfully affective ('moving') appeal of music—what one artist mentioned earlier calls "latching on."†

As briefly introduced earlier, aisthesis for Aristotle and the ancient Greeks is the source of knowledge gained through the bodily senses. Aisthesis, then, focuses attention on values that are ignored or denigrated by speculative-rationalist aesthetic theories, for example, those of phenomenology and pragmatism that acknowledge the importance of the body, and of sociocultural research dealing with the social meanings of the arts. The social importance of praxis, then, goes back to the beginnings of Western civilization as we know it today. It is not a newcomer in the social or philosophical theory of art and music. In consequence, it is decidedly rooted in a capital "P" philosophical heritage that is still widely admired.

. . .

Theoria for Contemplation

First, Aristotle distinguishes three kinds of knowledge and their respective uses. *Theoria* is speculative-rational knowledge, and its active form is *contemplation* (e.g., contemplating the 'beauty' of a mathematical proof). In this, it might seem to bear a close relationship to orthodox accounts of aesthetic contemplation. However, as noted in Part One, Ancient Greece made an important

74

distinction between the *sense-based* knowledge of aisthesis and the *rational* knowledge gained through reason.† Theoria (for Aristotle) is knowledge reached through reasoning about the eternal order of the cosmos and the will of the gods, not through the senses. It exists to be contemplated in leisure time as a prime source of happiness (*eudaimonia*).*

Speculative-rational aesthetic theory, instead, denies the strongly 'felt' attractions of aisthesis and extols only contemplation and claims to "aesthetic emotions" that are, somehow, not the 'real' emotions of life.† Thus, "sadness" in music is not that of, say, a funeral and thus we shouldn't cry upon hearing such music. We simply recognize (i.e., *re*-cognize in a musical setting) the musical presentation of the general (generic?) 'feel' of "sadness."

Notably, the philosophers in ancient Greece who created and contemplated theoria were a super-elite minority—much like today's "pure" scientists (or, for that matter, many of today's music theorists, aestheticians, "musicianists,"* and cognoscenti). In Aristotle's time, these scholars had little interest in the daily affairs of ordinary people—especially slaves and women. Nonetheless, they held the rational knowledge of theoria to be superior to aisthesis. The latter, they claimed, depended on the body and thus resulted in different particular experiences according to the subjective, bodily differences between individuals. In contrast, rational knowledge was thought to be certain, stable, and universally and timelessly valid.†

(Nevertheless, during the Enlightenment, Emmanuel Kant attempted to mediate the competing claims between sensation—aisthesis—and reason in his three famous critiques: *The Critique of Pure Reason* [1781], *The Critique of Practical Reason* [1788], and *The Critique of Judgment* [1790]. He thus initiated a "critical philosophy" that reviews and challenges all theories for their truth value instead of, as in earlier ages (e.g., Baumgarten and *Aesthetica*), making or justifying claims about truth and reality. Thus, his philosophy greatly qualified ideas of both pure reason and judgments of sense. This "critical" spirit is seen in the epigram of the present book.)

However, for Aristotle, some kinds of theory can be 'applied' with benefit to productive and utilitarian ends and can thus guide technical judgments. Such theory thus goes beyond its "pure" form and contemplative function by benefitting productive actions. At the most basic level of craftsmanship, productive actions are a matter of rigorously following the rules and traditions learned in an apprenticeship. However, in more complex situations, such traditional rules do not cover all the possibilities for deciding on action. Thus, *applied theory* can help guide the process of acting in such situations*—in particular, to notably creative ends, such as in the arts (e.g., color theory, harmonic theory, serialism, acoustics).

Techne and Artisanal Making

Aristotle's second kind of knowledge is *techne*—skill-related ('how to') knowledge and technique—and its active form is 'good' or 'excellent making' *(poiesis)*. Today we identify this with the basic craft skills of artisans mentioned in the previous paragraph. It largely involved making 'things', performances, or productions (e.g., dances, celebrations, feasts, public readings of poetry and literature) that were uncontroversial because they were widely accepted as useful, interesting, or needed. Past mistakes of techne contributed to improving the skills of a particular craft-field or artisan (e.g., "measure twice, cut once" for carpenters and seamstresses). But, since 'things' and not people were involved, they carried no *ethical* responsibility—beyond competently serving the needs promised to paying customers.

As with artisans throughout history, there were individual differences of technique and skill between makers. However, differences between artisans were not seen as matters of *personal expression*—which is why, for example (as mentioned in Part One), prior to the Renaissance, musicians and artists rarely took credit for their work by signing their names to their creations.† Techne, even today, deals therefore with knowledge and skill that are capable of being *systematized* and *passed on to others* by instruction, direction, or modeling.

In music, for example, "do it this way" or "it goes like this" are teaching traits of many pedagogues who teach by imitation. Other pedagogues focus on technique as though a goal of its own. Thus, technical drills are required that are separate from "the music" studied. While such skill-drill may build digital dexterity, the finger-patterning involved often makes transfer to actual music more difficult. For example, Mozart's piano *Sonata No. 16 in C* (KV 545; "Sonata facile") features a sequence of C major scales in measures 5–10; but each sequence begins on a different scale degree of the scale (6, then 5, 4, and 3) and is fingered starting with the thumb. This fingering is thus different from the C major scale that begins and ends with the thumb on the first scale degree.* Having practiced the fingering for the scale can complicate playing the actual music. Instead of such separate technical exercises, meeting the technical demands of music itself builds the necessary "digital" technique, but in the praxial context of particular musical needs.

Teachers who assign lots of boring skill-drills are typically perplexed (and sometimes irritated) by the question "What is the difference between a piano lesson and a music lesson?" Teaching *music* via piano (or any performance medium) is, for many teachers, a novel and even challenging conception. The distinction is important because it reveals a teacher's philosophy of what music 'is' and why it is taught. The answer makes a great deal of difference in how teaching and learning *music* progress (or not).

Teaching students merely to produce sounds on an instrument and read notes (i.e., where the score is considered "the music")† often fails to observe this important difference. And exhortations to "add feeling" don't help. Furthermore, musicians are often the first to complain about a performance they judge to be "unmusical" and technically mechanical (a matter only of facile fingers, it seems). But, they often don't have a convincing answer when pressed for details of what they consider to be "musical" music.

Consider how many lessons focus on technique as an *end* in itself, rather than as a *means* to serve musical goals. How many students are 'turned off' to the former because they were at first attracted by music's attractions? Beginners in music—especially young ones—predictably fail to see the relation between skill-drill and their eventual musical pleasures.† With such a disconnection between technique and pleasurable results, the skill-drill is done mechanically (as though for its own sake: e.g., scales as calisthenics),† and the effectiveness of their practicing therefore suffers.

In any case, practicing that lacks music-focused mindfulness (i.e., that is not carefully attentive to musical criteria and the musical ends in question) is usually inefficient and ineffective. Both conditions often lead to quitting lessons; and to adults who often observe, "I wish my parents had made me practice"—a comment that demonstrates a common view that practicing music is "work" rather than a form of *disciplined play*—like sports practices. Responsibility for practicing is seen—and this is certainly conveyed by many teachers as part of their "hidden curriculum"†—as a matter of disciplined *duty*, not as a reasonable, practical step to more capable and musical enjoyments. With young students, it is again useful to remember that we "play" music, not "work" it.

For youth engaged in sports, in contrast, the relevance to and the connection between practicing and improved play and its pleasures are usually very clear (as is also the case for learning computer skills or cell phone apps and any manner of activities related to other personal interests).† This *mindful connection* between technique, practice, and improved results and pleasures is too often missing in music studies. Instead, students practice to *fill time* (e.g., what some teachers call "the 210 club": 30 minutes a day, seven days a week), because they are expected to—not just by teachers but often by their parents.

This emphasis on the *quantity* of practice rather than the *quality* of practice also often inclines students to engage in bad (ineffective, even negative) practicing habits. For example, they very often practice too fast in their attempts to approximate the musical pleasures they seek (not minding the errors and stop-and-restart stumbles); slow practice doesn't sound enough like the music, nor does working steadfastly on difficult passages. Thus, the time "filled" is typically not 'good time' (i.e., worth-while).† And, progressively, meaningful practicing becomes more and more rare or more and more a filling (killing?) of time that is not musically valued or musically valuable to the student. Too often other personal interests replace students' original musical motivations.

Music teachers have a lot to learn from the motivations for practicing of self-taught amateurs (and those who follow online instruction). Their practicing is motivated by the desire for improvement, not by the anticipation of a critique at the next lesson. Their practicing is a *loving* form of participation (as is the case with amateur golfers who are always trying to do their best).† In contrast, when, for whatever reason, music lessons cease (or with graduation), too many students seem not to have discovered significant enough reasons to continue to practice. Thus, they quit practicing and playing.

Praxis and Prudence in Aristotle

Aristotle's third kind of knowledge is *praxis*. And his use of the term clearly sets it off from the term "practice" (the common meaning of which was explained in earlier chapters as an *automatic repetition* or *mechanical routine*: setting your alarm clock, taking attendance for a class, carrying an umbrella when rain is likely). Instead, in Aristotle's sense, praxis is a matter of actions undertaken in behalf of the needs of people. Its active form is called *phronesis*, or "practical wisdom." Praxis, for Aristotle, is a matter of virtuous action. Importantly, though, for Aristotle, "virtue" is understood in the sense of *excellent doing*, not simply as a matter of moral respectability.*

The typical English synonym for "praxis" is the word "action."† As understood by *action theory* in several disciplines, then, an "action" is distinguished from simple "activity" by being *goal directed* and not mechanical, automatic, routine, and so on.† An action's *virtue* (i.e., excellence) is therefore seen in the degree to which the goals at stake are attained for those being served.† Thus, "phronesis" is often translated (somewhat incompletely) as *prudence:* a farsighted ability to diagnose, consider, and advance certain ends for those served—as based on praxial 'know-how' from past experience.† It is especially a matter of being *caring* enough regarding the needs of those to be served (in our case students* and their musical and personal thriving) to be '*care*-full' in bringing about positive results concerning those needs. Such teaching is concerned, then, to avoid infective results or the failure to meet the musical and personal needs at stake and, most important, to "do no harm"—an ethical criterion.†

With praxis, then, the welfare or thriving of *people* is at stake, not the production of 'things' or events. Therefore, mistaken actions—actions that fail to be clearly beneficial for those who are the focus of teaching agency—*do* carry responsibilities for which the teacher may be held *ethically* accountable. Such actions, particularly those that not only fail to help but that worsen the situated needs at stake, amount to *mal-praxis*: what in some professions is (legally) called "malpractice"—especially if repeatedly employed without attempts at overcoming predictable failure.†

A professional ethic in any field is one of *standards of care*, not "standard care."† And professional "practice" in, say, medicine, therapy, or dentistry is obviously not a matter of "practicing" on patients; it is entirely an ethical matter of '*care*-full' praxis, as Aristotle promoted long ago in his treatises on ethics. (For the same reason, "practice teaching" as a term has given way to a variety of euphemisms, such as "teaching internship" or "teaching practicum" and the like—even though it often seems to amount to "practicing" on students.)

Accordingly, philosophically and sociologically, praxis is any 'doing' or action that involves and serves people in a way that takes *their* needs, wants, and desires into consideration as a pragmatic guide to what is to be done in their behalf (e.g., the diagnostic praxis of a doctor). The need—or 'good-for'—in question, then, serves as both the pragmatic and, hence, the *ethical criteria* of success for *eupraxis* (i.e., successful praxis, such as whether the patient or student is helped; see, e.g., the epigram for this chapter).†

As praxis, teaching is not, therefore, to be equated with common "practices" that have no such ethical criteria and are just the routines and 'delivery-methods' and 'delivery-lessons' of teachers who go through the motions as though their classes and ensembles were like bus routes: a predictable itinerary, but with different passengers over time. Such teachers (in any subject) 'burn out' and quit. Or, worse, they 'burn in' and fixate on what gets them through the day or school year. They don't quit; they just live in a deadened life of comfortable and predictable teaching routines—routines they are contentedly familiar with, even when they often lead to predictable learning problems (e.g., "I taught it to them, but they didn't learn it") and to episodes of impolite and dysfunctional class behavior.

Aside from such common "discipline problems" shared with other classes, music education has its own species: for example, lack of practicing, talking or not paying attention in rehearsals, coming late to rehearsals, engaging in "off-task behavior" in music classes, and the like.

Every teacher has undoubtedly had such going-through-the-motions teachers (or professors) in their education careers. However, they often struggle to recognize the same tendency in their own teaching to fall into comfortable routines that are unresponsive to students' learning. Consider, in comparison, the apocryphal example of the teacher who complained to a colleague, "I taught it to them, but they didn't understand. So, I taught it to them a different way, but they still didn't understand. Then I taught it to them a third way, and, finally, I understood!" Such is the action research nature of *critically self-reflective* teaching praxis.†

It should be clear, then, that praxis in the Aristotelian sense is much more complex and ethically focused than are references to mere "practices." Parents feed their children and look after their immediate needs, but the praxis of responsible, loving parenthood is more than just that. Music teachers may teach music reading (and so on), but teaching *music* goes well beyond that!† And serving students' musical needs for their musical futures is certainly more than a routine matter of putting on the next concert, endlessly singing rote songs in classroom music, or 'delivering' the same formulaic lesson plans over the years.

Accordingly, the next concert should be much more consequential for students and their long-term development as musicians than just playing the correct notes, at the right time, as preprogrammed by the director's musical decisions and dictates. Parents look to the future of their children (we hope). But, too many music teachers focus on the details of 'pulling off' the next concert. They overlook the fact that the attention of the audience of parents is on their children, not in the aesthetic qualities of the performance. (A principal who admittedly had little musical training said that he mainly notices whether students are smiling and enjoying themselves more than he does the performance. I didn't ask him how students are supposed to smile with instruments in their mouths.)

And worse; in addition to asserting that a 'good concert' automatically amounts (somehow) to a 'good' (aesthetic) education, a single-minded focus on the next concert too often fails to promote long-term curricular consequences for students' musical growth and *independent musicianship*. Similarly, 'delivering' a formulaic lesson plan, no matter how smoothly, does not mean that music learning has been effective or lasting. With teachers who go through the motions, their students also often go through the motions, mindless (lacking intentionality)† of any musical growth. Thus, while they seem active, even interested (not always a reliable sign of learning), they are only going along without any musical or learning goals in mind. Any benefits are short term.

As a result, the "curriculum" often only 'exposes' students to "experiences" and classroom "activities" and, in ensembles, to x-years of concert literature. Commonly, then, music teachers often refer to "my [our] program" but not to "my [our] curriculum." Student teachers or administrators who ask about "the curriculum" are given abundant "words" of advocacy in support of "the program." These usually amount to recitals of the same claims made by their aesthetic advocacy, extolling their "high standards" and claiming that "the program" is thriving.

Aside, then, from the usual school concerts and abundant "activities" in classroom music, "the program" (again, as compared to a bus route)† too often fails to have promoted functionally independent musicianship that prepares students for a fully active life of amateur musicking. In the minds of the public and administrators, the few graduates who intend to go on to professional careers in music fail to warrant the trouble and expense of mounting school music ensembles. (How expensive is a quality tuba these days? Such costs rival those of extracurricular sports and only add to the legitimation crisis of school music.)

Praxis in Contemporary Society and Culture

Sociologically and anthropologically, a society is formed or structured in important ways by the vast network of social interactions and communities of praxis in which members typically engage: (a) religion, work, sports, art, music, language, food, manners, customs, and traditions; and (b) social *institutions* such as government, marriage, schooling, professions, law, politics, banking, even money. The ideology supporting a social praxis shapes individuals at the same time that individuals shape society over time according to changing conditions and evolving needs. (Recall the discussion in the Introduction of situations where an "ideology" is in force—or enforced—when either a system of ideas is at stake or—more problematically—the values of a dominant social group are imposed on others).†

Among such ever-changing conditions to which an institutional ideology needs to respond are transformations over time in the conditions that motivated the original praxis. Institutions that cope well with such changing social conditions and needs are the central means by which society and culture are educated, reproduced, and advanced. Praxis is the 'glue' that holds together everyday social formations and communities of this kind.* However, a legitimation crisis† such as that which challenges school music today is typically the result of not keeping up with changing times. Music and musicking have changed rapidly in recent years, whereas many teachers still operate on aesthetic pretensions that have been bypassed in the world of music.

For contemporary *neo-Marxian sociology* (i.e., a classical sociological theory, not the political or economic social policy of Marxism or communism—a crucial distinction*) and associated Critical Theory, however, praxis is the action of a person who attempts to change the surrounding lifeworld for the better. Unlike the Aristotelian focus of praxis on the needs of a particular group (e.g., students, parishioners, patients), such actions attempt not to *reproduce* that lifeworld but to *improve it* for the betterment of all people. The intent, then, is to profit one's own life and, potentially, by extension, the lives of others.* Communities of praxis† (i.e., institutions) socially magnify the efforts of individuals through collective efforts at change and progress.

Originally, praxis in this sense was understood simply as "labor." But, understood more broadly in classical sociology, praxis involves the personal or social needs and 'goods' served by the practices of an existing sociocultural structure.* Or it involves a social institution or praxis that comes into being to serve a *new* social need. The invention in the nineteenth century of formal schooling is a good example of a new institutional praxis evolving to serve a newly recognized social need. And differences between societies are seen in the different communities of praxis they adopt for common or similar social needs. Thus, all modern societies have schools, but their schooling praxis differs in key ways—how schools are built and run, what is taught, to what social, personal, economic, and political ends or purposes, how teaching and learning are evaluated, and so on.

Sociologists of music, ethnomusicologists, and cultural anthropologists all understand the praxis of "music" in its plural forms. Thus, as briefly noted in Part One,† "musics" are to "music" what different "languages" to are to "language" or "laws" are to the "law": the multiple and always context-situated praxial forms summarized by the collective noun. These disciplines all agree that the praxis of music helps to define and hold together a society (or cultural group), as well as to define and identify (even interpenetrate, as with crossover musics) the various subcultures and segments of any sociocultural entity. And music is widely responsible for conferring identity on the members of communities of musical praxis.

The habit of referring to "music" (as collective noun) already hypothesizes some *common* ground among all musics in the world. Recognizing their *differences* and the *distinct social values* of each, however, is a special feature of a praxial perspective. To be precise, the differences among musics in terms of their social contributions, contexts, and components are so great that "music" education should rightfully be "musics" education.† However, the collective noun will suffice as long as the rich plurality of its forms is appropriately recognized as the basis for music education and not just the musics 'high' on the aesthetic hierarchy.

Music, accordingly, is shaped by society at the same time that its evolution and development help shape and reflect society—thus accounting for musical differences among societies and for the praxis of different musical subcultures within a society. "Music" is therefore not a singular 'thing', a canon or collection of autonomous 'works'. Instead, it is a wide and ever-expanding range of *living* praxis: an active, functional, and endless source of social 'doings' via musical sounds and formats that have cultural importance beyond 'sounding forms' for their own sake. The 'sounding forms' of praxis are, instead, a central form of human agency by which both personal and communal lives are constituted and lived.†

In Part One the conditions of a praxial theory of music were said to concern what music 'is', what the nature of its existence in the world is.† In a praxial sense, *music* (in all its many forms) comes into existence when (a) status, meaning, and value are (b) added by social agreement (society) (c) to sounds created, selected, and organized (d) to serve socially important personal and social needs and 'goods'. Or, the reverse: when sounds are selected and organized in ways that reveal and serve ("make special") socially important occasions.† Think about that description for long enough to realize that its implications for music as social praxis are great.

This account of music parallels the way in which the praxis and institution of "money" (or, recently, "bitcoins" in the digital world) are (a) value added by society (b) to pieces of paper and metal (c) that are created and organized (d) to serve important socioeconomic needs. In the same sense, then, particular sociopersonal and cultural needs and goods contribute meaning to the musical sounds in question, and vice versa. (And we surely pay keen attention to the social meanings of those pieces of paper and coins.)

"Music," thus, is a *social function added by a society, individual, or group to sounds* in relation to the use of those sounds as chosen and organized for particular 'goods' or needs.* This includes, then, everything from music for audience listening, religion, entertainment, ceremonies, celebrations, and recreation to music for advertising, film, TV, and commercial uses. In fact, any society or culture is constituted in part through and is constantly lived by means of an unlimited number of musical traditions that continue to evolve, particularly as recordings and new media lead to the rapid spread and evolution of musics.† For example, consider the piano accompaniments to silent films, then the rise of film music, then of music for television, leading to music videos and video art that includes music, and you can understand how music is continually evolving new forms of praxis, finding new uses, creating new social realities.

Ponder, as well, the incredibly numerous social meanings and 'goods' served by the new musics of the twentieth and twenty-first centuries: 'popular' musics as well as those that aspire to presentational art forms. We may well wonder if Beethoven, Brahms, or Bach would even recognize or appreciate the abundance of musics today as "music" (e.g., the Beatles, Brubeck, and be-bop, or Berg, Bartok, and Boulez).† Yet, in fact, many who are tied to the aesthetic theory of art deny the status or social importance of these newer musics for contemporary life. In fact, ever since the rise of the avant-garde in the early twentieth century (or perhaps earlier), the aesthetic ideology has been under siege by modern artists in all fields.*

It is fair to say that today's music teachers have grown up in an expanded world of "musics" and accept and appreciate them (as even more and more music professors do, though they may be reluctant to reflect it profession-ally). Yet, in their teaching, they often follow the influences and outlines of the aesthetic ideology into which they were socialized in school as university music students. Fortunately, their more widespread musical interests and skills make them especially receptive to a praxial persuasion if only they could go (or grow) beyond the all-too-evident limitations and dysfunctions for school music of the typical aesthetic model.

Related Readings

C.D.C. Reeve. *Action, Contemplation and Happiness: An Essay on Aristotle*. Cambridge, MA: Harvard University Press, 2012.

An in-depth study of theoria in Aristotle's writing. See p. 140 for the epigram to this chapter.

Thomas A. Regelski. "Musicianism and the Ethics of School Music." *Action, Criticism, and Theory for Music Education* 11(1): 7–42.

A " musicianist" is a teacher who puts the sacralized aesthetic ideology before students' musical needs and interests.

Measures 5–10 of Mozart's *Sonata facile*: http://dme.mozarteum.at/DME/nma/nma_cont.php?vsep=197&gen=edition&l=1&p1=122 (accessed May 15, 2015).

C.D.C. Reeve. *Aristotle on Practical Wisdom*. Cambridge, MA: Harvard University Press, 2013.

A definitive study of practical wisdom in Aristotle.

Joseph Dunne. *Back to the Rough Ground: 'Phronesis' and 'Techne' in Modern Philosophy and Aristotle*. Notre Dame: University of Notre Dame Press, 1993.

A very useful study of these two central concepts; one of the best scholarly sources.

Nel Noddings. *The Challenge to Care in Schools: An Alternative Approach to Education*, 2nd ed. New York: Teachers College Press, 2005.

An example of phronesis as a criterion for teachers.

Hans Joas. "A Sociological Transformation of the Philosophy of Praxis: Anthony Giddens Theory of Structuration." In H. Joas, *Pragmatism and Social Theory*. Chicago: University of Chicago Press, 1993; 172–187.

An account of praxis philosophy in non-Aristotelian and modern sociological terms and in opposition to functionalism. See also Chapter Six, "Institutionalization as a Creative Process," pp. 154–171.

Thomas A. Regelski. "Action Learning: Curriculum and Instruction as and for Praxis." In Marie McCarthy, ed., *Music Education as Praxis*. College Park: University of Maryland, 1999; 97–120.

George Ritzer. *Sociological Theory*, 3rd ed. New York: McGraw-Hill, 1983.
For neo-Marxian sociology, pp. 41–71.

C. Calhoun, J. Gerteis, J. Moody, S. Pfaff, K. Schmidt, and I. Virk. *Classical Sociological Theory*. Oxford: Blackwell, 2005.
For neo-Marxian sociology, pp. 19–102.

Richard Kilminster. *Praxis and Method: A Sociological Dialogue with Lukacs, Gramsci, and the Early Frankfurt School*. Boston: Routledge and Kegan Paul, 1979.
A history of early Critical Theory in social philosophy.

Jüergen Habermas. *Theory and Practice*. Boston: Beacon Press, 1973.
The relation between social, political, and economic theory and praxis.

Michel de Certeau. *The Practice of Everyday Life*. Berkeley: University of California Press, 1988.
A classic.

Raimo Tuomela. *The Philosophy of Social Practices: A Collective Acceptance View.* Cambridge: Cambridge University Press, 2002.
A philosophy of social practice (and therefore somewhat different from a sociological study).

Pierre Bourdieu. *The Logic of Practice*. Trans R. Nice. Stanford: Stanford University Press, 1990.
A classic sociological study.

Pierre Bourdieu. *Practical Reason: On the Theory of Action*. Stanford: Stanford University Press, 1998.
Another classic study from a leading sociologist.

Pierre Bourdieu and Jean-Claude Passeron. *Reproduction in Education, Society and Culture*, 2nd ed. London: SAGE, 1990.
How schooling transmits social distinctions and ideologies.

Thomas A. Regelski. "Musical Values and the Value of Music Education." *Philosophy of Music Education Review* 10(1) (Spring 2002): 49–55.
Concerning "music" as a value added by society to sound that serves social needs and purposes.

Peter Bürger. *Theory of the Avant-Garde*. Trans. M. Shaw. Minneapolis: University of Minneapolis Press, 2009.
See especially Chapter Three "Problem of the Autonomy of Art in Bourgeois Society" and "The Negation of the Autonomy of Art by the Avant-Garde."

6

PRAXIS IN MUSIC AND MUSIC EDUCATION

*Practical wisdom [**phronesis**] . . . is concerned with human affairs and what can be deliberated about; for of a practically wise man we say that this most of all is the function, to deliberate well, and nobody deliberates about what cannot be otherwise or about the sorts of things that do not lead to some specific end **(telos ti)**, where this is something good, doable in action. The unconditionally good deliberator, however, is the one capable of aiming, in accord with calculation, at the best, for a human being, of things doable in action.*
Aristotle (trans. C.D.C. Reeve)

In music and music education, the term "praxis," as its application in music education is approached here and as a recommended action or generative ideal,† refers to *three* different sets of inextricably interrelated conditions. Each set (indicated in bold font) is considered from the perspective of music educators (i.e., teachers, but also professors, music administrators, and so on) and students. These conditions and their implications account for the many ways in which "praxis" can be distinguished from reference to the common sense of "practice" and to the critique of music education that relies on the ideology of the aesthetic theory of art and the ideology of aesthetic education. Those interested in understanding praxis as an alternative to the aesthetic theory of music and art should be guided in their deliberations about the good and doable ends of teaching by these three important criteria for a music education that is informed by praxial conditions and criteria.

. . .

Praxis as a Noun

(1) First, as a **noun**, praxis promotes a notable *result* accomplished or produced.

Music, in this sense, is a *product* or end result (*telos*) created to serve certain social or personal circumstances, conditions, and needs. Thus, different social or practical needs—according to the society, culture, or subculture—account for the existence of and differences among various musics (e.g., concert music, dance music, religious music, dinner music, film music, background/mood/party music, patriotic music). They then become occasions for the continuing use of that music thereafter—or that *kind* of music as it evolves over time (e.g., what is 'popular' at a given time).

The 'goodness' or quality of such music is judged in terms how well the particular human purposes, individuals, or groups at stake are pragmatically served by the musical praxis (e.g., 'good for' concert listening, dancing, worship), not by abstract claims of 'for-itself' grounds. Good health, for example, is not an absolute ('for-itself') singular quality; it is judged in terms that are particular to each person's unique condition. So, too, 'good music' is valued only according to the needs and 'goods' served by the particular musical human needs at stake. For example, a jazz band hired to play dance music may play music that is 'good for' listening but may not be 'good for' dancing (e.g., is too fast, changes meters). Conversely, music that is 'good for' dancing is often not 'good for' concert listening (i.e., it fails to offer enough details of musical interest to profit audience listening). Thus, the 'good-for' or pragmatic need being served provides the criteria by which the 'goodness' of the music in question is judged. Such pragmatic criteria, then, eliminate the criticism of "anything goes" *relativism*. Instead, 'goodness' is seen empirically in the pragmatic 'goods' (good ends) actually achieved.

For **music educators**, praxis as a noun requires conceiving of curriculum goals, outcomes, and end results that will be tangibly *observable* and notably *pragmatic* in nature. Curriculum is therefore calculated on the need to *make a difference* in the "value added" sense of the 'goods' or values that curriculum exists to advance, enhance, or improve.* 'Bus route'† kinds of routine teaching only pass the time, usually to the discomfort of both students and teachers.

As regards **students**, successful teaching praxis† is best seen in what students are musically *able to* and *want to do*—newly or at all (e.g., read music), better, more often, or more enthusiastically, more rewardingly—as a result of instruction. The advancement of such musical praxis is (a) the formal difference music education *adds* to the informal music education students bring with them to school; (b) the musical value *added* to students' present lives and the potential of such musical value for the life well lived; and (c) the musical value *added* by school graduates to social and cultural practices that come into being in connection with music. As introduced earlier, music is "performative" not only in the sense that it is performed: Music is *performative* because it literally *creates* social realities that previously did not exist (e.g., concerts, dances, celebrations).* Musical praxis and its 'products' are thus central ingredients in the "performance" of sociality and culture via music—and not just 'high' culture.†

Praxis as Action

(2) Second, praxis as a **verb form** refers to an action—or, more accurately, to act*ing*.

Thus, in music, praxis is a 'do*ing*', or a try*ing* to of a *musical* kind (or at least to which music is central). The verb form is the sense of "musicking"† as active praxis, not as a museum collection of 'works'. Such 'doing' of music is its own reward. As we have already seen, an *action* is distinguished from mere *activity* by the intentions or goals that guide action.† Mere activities, instead, are usually habitual, from setting your alarm clock to consulting bus routes. The *intentionality* of an action involves, in contrast, keen attention to the musical goals and purposes that it is 'about' or 'for', that it is directed towards accomplishing. Mere "activity," in comparison, lacks this 'aboutness' and is often only an automatic response or an ingrained habit: a routine, a mere behavior, an impulse, an involuntary reaction (scratching where it itches or adjusting your eyeglasses).*†

Many activities of classroom (general) music lack this *musical* 'aboutness': the mindful desire and goal on the part of students to accomplish new musical skills that will serve the pleasures of improved praxis. Or their intentionality is only 'about' having fun with music (e.g., a 'fun' break from other studies). Thus, such activities often fail to promote any long-term *musical* benefits, skills, and long-term dispositions.† Music teachers of classroom music are usually the first to take note of when and how what used to be 'fun' activities in earlier years lead to various forms of nonconforming or reluctant behavior (i.e., "discipline problems"). This condition arises when students, usually pre-pubescent nine- to twelve-year-old "tween-agers" (i.e., the development stage between childhood and the teenage years) no longer take seriously the previously 'fun' activities of music classes.*

In music, praxis involves an endless range of musical 'doings': performative social undertakings or occasions that exist only as a result of the 'doing' of the music.† Concerts for audience listening are examples of social events brought into being by the use of music (and requiring musical complexity that invites listening interest and pleasure). But so are drumming circles, sing-alongs (such as Christmas caroling), karaoke, creating a particular party mood through well-chosen music, use of music in aerobics and jogging (e.g., matters of tempo, pacing, and energetic inspiration), dance music (including ballet and modern dance), music therapy, worshiping and praying through music, celebrations, rites, and rituals of all kinds. The list of such musicking is endless and growing in today's modern age of media.

A reminder, here, that 'music appreciation', understood as praxis,† is thus seen only in action; it is not some hypothesized and unseen psychological state of mind or cognitive state. It is empirically qualified by how, when, where, and why music is used pragmatically in enhancing life and enriching society.* The verb form "musicking" was coined to stress this active, praxial 'doing'. Accordingly, "musicking" has the same active relation to "music" as "loving" does to "love": If love is best seen in the loving actions it promotes, then music appreciation is seen in the loving musicking it promotes! Thus, 'music appreciation' does not depend on some kind preliminary informational stage that needs to be studied and mastered on the way to a love of music; it is already a sign of intimate (i.e., loving, 'felt') experience with music!*

However, as has been repeatedly stressed, musicking is equated not only with performing, listening, or composing but with all forms of active engagement with music and music-related topics and actions—for example, pursuing interests in the history of a musical genre, following particular artists on social media, collecting CDs and other recorded music, hi-fi interests, music criticism, and the like. And, clearly, today's youth have access to ever-new music apps for musicking that go well beyond typical aesthetic conditions of performing, composing, and listening. And the future will bring ever-more new technology and media for musical praxis not yet even envisaged!

Music teaching as and for praxis, then, is a process of stressing and promoting students' *mindfulness* (intentionality) for making and learning music—rather than mindless activity (e.g., just routinely obeying a director's musical judgments and tastes or going along with 'fun' musical activities). Approached from a praxial perspective, teaching avoids rote learning, memorization, or definitions of musical terms for their own sake or as an academic discipline. It seeks not to 'fill' a mind with abstract concepts (the "banking theory" of music education: the assumption that students' minds are like empty bank accounts that need to be filled from outside with value). It seeks to light a fire of desire and commitment for music.

The objective, then, is not to "experience" (as the aesthetics motivated lingo goes) what a concept or term *is* or is *about*. The objective is what it *does* in musical praxis and how, when, and why to *do* or *use* it! Its 'aboutness' is learning what music *is* and *is 'good for'* by directly undergoing what music *does* and *how* and *why* it does so. A concept *learned* is thus seen in what it *accomplishes musically*; it is a skill, a 'doing' not an abstract idea. Learning the "concept of melody," for example, is not having "experienced" the verbal abstraction via musical "activities." It entails the ability to *use* melody, respond to melodies, create melodies, and connect 'feelingfully' with melodies and their various transformations and particulars in a composition. Thus, concept learning is not a matter of exemplifying ("experiencing") the meaning of words and terms (e.g., "love) but of praxial engagement, of doing. Concept learning is learned through and seen in action (e.g., "loving). (Parent to child: "I will hug you as an experience of the concept of love"?)

As regards **students**, the verb form of music praxis involves their actively looking forward to (the intentionality of) *improving* the musical rewards and pleasures at stake in a lesson. They seek to improve their skills, learn new literature, widen their social community of musicking colleagues, and otherwise expand their musical choices and horizons. The verb form also involves reflect*ing* on their musical actions with the conscious intention of maintaining or increasing competence and pleasures or of extending competence to new applications (e.g., new chords or strums) or musical domains (e.g., new repertoire or styles). Practicing that is not fully mindful in this regard amounts merely to mindless activity, to mere repetition.†

Under such conditions, students do not progress mindfully—fully aware of the "virtuous" (i.e., excellent) results to be sought. This distracts them from practicing (at all, enough, or well), or they quit study altogether for lack of musical growth and musical rewards.† As we have seen, understanding the importance of goal directedness and 'aboutness' while practicing music is benefited by comparisons with young people's practicing of various interests and activities undertaken for their rewards (e.g., composition software, music apps). These they practice (i.e., study) for the rewards of getting better, and they continue to practice even more in order to enjoy those rewards. Why are the motivation and learning process that advance such student interests so mysterious to some music teachers? (Parent to child: "It's time to practice your apps.")

Praxis, in the verb sense, also involves students *acting adaptively* according to changing musical needs—their changing personal needs or the needs of the particular situations to be served musically—and to ever-new musical choices (e.g., performing in new keys, composing more coherent and interesting songs). Most important, their musicking involves *creating* their personal musical lives, their musical Selves, their personhood, and thus their personal musical histories through their musical choices and intentions. By its very nature, their musicking evolves throughout life as life itself undergoes changes—physical, social, economic, and so on. Considerable scholarship identifies and investigates, for example, the relation between music and personal, social, and cultural identity and meaning:* the role of music in confirming who "I" am, *my* attributes, interests, and values.

Praxial Knowledge

(3) Third, praxis also generates **practical (praxial) knowledge**.*

Praxial knowledge is the pragmatic 'know how', 'how to', and 'can do' that arise only from the verb form of praxis—from musicking.† Praxial knowledge thus arises in direct connection with the results of the (already praxial) conditions of a specific musical praxis as a noun; from excellent musical results for a particular praxis. Importantly, then, knowledge *for* praxis develops *from* praxis, **not** as a *precondition* of praxis. Facts, information, theory, concepts, and so on are developed *through* and *in* action (through doing), not as some kind of abstract (verbal) information or preliminary understanding claimed to be needed *before* one can begin to engage in a praxis. (Note: Learning to use chopsticks is a matter of using chopsticks to eat or else going hungry, not "It's time to practice using your chopsticks.") Regular *use* that contends with ever-new conditions of excellence, then, is the virtue in *practicing* any praxis.

Praxial knowledge, therefore, always takes the form of *skill*. Such practical knowledge can be and usually is applied to various purposes. It is *used*, not just memorized and forgotten. Through regular use under various situated conditions, praxial knowledge grows in effectiveness and through use. Riding a bicycle is an example.

Praxial knowledge is also *embodied*; thus, the knowledge for 'doing' music resides somewhat differently in each unique body. Just as the body learns to ride a bicycle or ski, we acquire a functional knowledge of key signatures, time signatures, and the like through use (which is why we are more comfortable with keys and meters we use the most; like me, you're probably not easily familiar with compositions in seven sharps or flats). Such knowledge becomes a functional, praxial skill to the degree it regularly gets *used* and thus, like riding a bicycle, is never forgotten. To help learn the "concept of balance," we engage learners in situations that progressively develop and refine the *bodily knowing* involved: walking, skiing, biking, gymnastics, musicking, and the like.

Yet music teachers can easily fall into the trap of giving *examples* of this or that verbal concept—usually in pursuit of exemplifying the so-called "elements of music"—melody, harmony, rhythm, form, and timbre—or the meaning of "counterpoint," "augmentation," "development," and other academic terms in music. Typically, however, praxial knowledge cannot usually be easily or effectively put into *words*. Thus, lectures with information 'about' music are futile, like advising a child who is learning to ride a bicycle to "keep your balance"! A similar situation in music is to "play in tune" or "add feeling." Such learning requires praxial conditions in various contexts over time (e.g., the "blue notes" of jazz intonation are usually not typical outside jazz and 'popular' musics).

Progress and achievement are thus demonstrated in action, through so-called *authentic assessment*. The authentic musical praxis at stake serves as both the curricular goal and the criterion for assessing both teaching accountability and learning. Fingering of instruments is not a matter of paper-and-pencil tests; it is 'tested' by actually playing the correct notes. Teaching swimming is clearly a matter of increasing praxial proficiency, not teaching the "concept" of staying afloat. And because it takes form differently in different bodies, praxial knowledge is *existentially personalized* as *"my* knowledge," because *my* body and its experiences are unique. It becomes part of *my* Self: *"I* am a music lover," *"I* sing in a choir," *"I* collect CDs," *"I* love jazz," *"I* play piano," *"I* programmed *my* playlist," "I follow my favorite artists and musics," *"I* can swim," and the like.

Technical abilities (i.e., techne) are best acquired directly from the authentic musical praxis rather than through the drilling of isolated skills.† Imagine teaching bicycle riding by dwelling on isolated, preliminary physical skills (e.g., individual lessons focused on steering, pedaling, braking, and "keeping your balance"). Again, competency is achieved only by means of engaging in the holistic praxis of riding a bicycle, and good teaching plans for developing musical skills involve various ways of engaging the child in the praxis by gradual stages.

Of course, when the very young are learning to ride a bicycle, they are very motivated with the 'aboutness' of keeping their balance, propelling themselves, and being able to steer and stop. In comparison, in music education, skill-drill is of little value when done without the 'aboutness' of a musical context or purpose, as though for its own sake. And when transfer of skill to holistic, authentic praxis is imperfect or nonexistent, the results are too often pedagogically negative.† Then, students who are forced to practice skill-drills apart from musical contexts quit lessons out of boredom because they want to play *music*, not scales and uninteresting unmusical exercises. It is the music and their desire to 'make' it at higher and more rewarding levels that interested them to begin with.†

Skill-drill isolated from musical conditions can often be blamed for dulling and extinguishing this initial enthusiasm for musicking. It is *an*esthetic and musically inert! (A composer friend used to criticize his violinist wife—who played in a notable orchestra—for not playing her "scales" and so on "musically"—no doubt a reason why they're no longer married.) No less a performing artist than the pianist and conductor Daniel Barenboim, certainly one of the superstars of the 'classical' music world, reflects a praxis-based pedagogy:

> I studied with my father till I was about seventeen. For me learning to play the piano was as natural as learning to walk. My father had an obsession about wanting things to be natural. I was brought up on the fundamental principle that there is no division between musical and technical problems. This was an integral part of his philosophy. I was never made to practice scales or arpeggios [only] the pieces themselves. . . . My father's teaching was based on the belief that there are enough scales in Mozart's concertos.*

Or, as seen in the last chapter, there are plenty of scales in Mozart's sonatas (along with much else that benefits techne).† Choosing interesting music that "practices" technique in and for selected musical contexts is a pedagogically holistic approach, just as the use of "etudes" is with advanced students. It is all the better if a variety of musics is studied, thus allowing the student to develop general musicianship that can serve an assortment of musics.

Practicing music, when itself qualified by the conditions, contexts, and criteria of mindful musical praxis, is thus different from merely repeating passages mechanically, routinely, or unmusically (What is the equivalent of arpeggios for bicycling competence?). Practicing music is no more a matter of fulfilling a requirement to practice so many minutes or hours a day than is practicing to learn how to ride a bike or to ski according to set periods of time. (Imagine a child announcing, "I'm going to practice riding my bicycle.")

Instead, practicing is a loving but disciplined 'play' that is fully *mindful* of what is required to reach intended results.† In the case of music, these are musically playful results valuable in their own sake and in terms of the intention to meet the musical needs, purposes, and rewards at stake. From a praxial perspective, musical intentionality is a matter of intending to learn, to progress, or to solve a musical problem or achieve a musical aspiration.

Practicing is always importantly guided by an (informed) *aural image* of the intended musical result.† Only then are mistakes (of notes, technique, style, phrasing, expression, or anything else that detracts from effective musical results) noticed, addressed, and remedied by the student. A teacher is thus responsible for helping students, first of all, to have an aural image (of everything from good tone, intonation, and phrasing to tempo, dynamics, and the like) and then for establishing the conditions by which that image can be fulfilled. One reason that very young students of the Suzuki method play so musically seems to be the aural image they get from the recorded models provided to them from the earliest years of study.

At a certain point, of course, a musical *norm* (standard) stressed at first by the teacher can be extended creatively. But, too often, the image given students is that of some idea of "standard" praxis—often concerning only accurate execution of the score.† This confusion of "standard" praxis and "standards of care" (seen earlier in connection with ethics) thus creates a false criterion of "standards" by which much of the assessment of student musicians is judged. Of course, it is not unreasonable for students to be taught to be attentive to the norms of a particular praxis. But the danger is that such standards are those only of the teacher (or professor)—who, after all, isn't usually subject to the reviews of the competitive music marketplace—or who is focused only on "standard" values, such as the next concert or recital. The fascination with "standards" (and the constant rhetoric about upholding "high standards") seems to be an unwieldy premise for musical creativity or for serving the musical interests of either student performers or the audiences of professional artists.

In any case, *how to practice* most efficiently and effectively is rarely taught (or learned).† Thus, when students waste much time and fail to make musically rewarding progress, they often lose interest and quit. In sum, the playing and practicing of music, like the playing and practicing of sports, is not simply a matter of fun or fooling around. Instead, it is a matter of intentional and disciplined striving to attain important goals—in sports, of course, developing competence enough to enjoy the competitive play; in music, striving to reach a personally rewarding musical result.†

If we consider why it is commonly said that we "play" music, we should consider the drudgery (or work ethos) imposed by "no pain, no gain" pedagogies (e.g., see in particular the 2015 film *Whiplash*, which, despite portraying the obvious ethical deficiencies of such a pedagogical *pathology*, concludes by seeming to confirm it. Many musicians can confirm, from personal experience, the ethical and pedagogical dilemma of pedagogical *tyrants*.). Musicking should be 'play' in all its forms, no matter how 'serious' the occasion. The play of children, in fact, always involves a serious focus and intense concentration (and imagination) that music teachers ought to pay more attention to and encourage.

A strong focus on highly competitive teaching strategies (e.g., for seating, solos, lead roles) not only masks the play element in music but also too often creates a cadre of 'losers' whose *intrinsic* musical play impulse and pleasure are thus shut down and denied validity in favor of the *extrinsic* goal of winning or recognition. It is a shame that so many beginning students are 'turned off' to the playfulness of musicking by teachers for whom music is a discipline pursued in pursuit of the aesthetic theory of art. Paradoxically, while pursuing the aesthetic ideal, such teachers instead destroy students' initial musical motivations, their 'intimacy' with music. In their enthusiasm for what they understand to be aesthetic standards, they too often destroy a student's enthusiasm for musics that have initially interested them praxially and that they want to 'do' more often and better.

As regards *praxial knowledge* from the perspective of **music teaching** as praxis, then, the overriding goal is to motivate *musical independence*: praxial knowledge that can be put into loving, playful practice by students and graduates, independent of a teacher or other guide. *Standards* of success or quality are judged according to the objective needs and other criteria of the musical practices at stake (e.g., good wedding music, good music for leisure-time listening, good dance music, good jazz, good Beethoven, 'good for' an aerobics workout or party).

But standards of meaningful praxis also vary according to the interests, needs, criteria, and present skills of the practitioner. Thus, there are relevant differences in ability, expectations, and intentionality between children and adults and between amateurs and professionals. Standards also vary according to the 'goods' at stake for a particular musical praxis. Thus, the praxis of performing as an amateur for one's own pleasure is different from the praxis expected of performing for an audience (Einstein is said to have played violin but resisted performing for others, and he wasn't stupid). And the standards for the praxis of a church choir in the worship service are different from those for those same singers if presenting a public concert for audience listening.

By definition, 'good music' and 'good time' from musicking will differ according to the conditions of the situation—amateur, professional, or a variety of in-between practices. A group of professors who regularly gathered *socially* to drink beer and wine and sing naughty catches and glees quickly vetoed a suggestion that they give a concert. A presentational concert would have required rehearsing, and their musical rewards were instead participatory (or perhaps they considered that concert choirs don't consume alcohol on stage).

Teaching that promotes independent praxial musical knowledge and long-term positive dispositions on the part of students is reflective, diagnostic, and adaptive. It approximates the *action research* briefly mentioned in Chapter Five.† Rather than 'adopting' formulaic 'delivery-methods', action research helps teachers continually seek to improve the actual functional musical results of their teaching praxis. For action research, teaching is always *problematized*, always seen as a 'problem' condition that can never be 'good enough', that can always be improved through *systematic* experimentation and study.

Teaching methods (didactics) and materials are thus regarded as 'tools' that serve to actually advance the musical praxis of students; they are not otherwise valued for their own sake, in advance, as though they were one-size-fits-all teaching technologies (i.e., techne). As with the tools of any field, a teaching 'tool' is as good as (a) what it is 'good for' building, (b) how effectively it is used, and (c) the tangible 'goods' it actually produces, or 'what' is built. Too often, 'delivery-methods'—no matter how well 'delivered'—are 'tools' that produce little or nothing of lasting musical merit.† A single-minded focus on 'delivering' the *method* or 'canned' lesson can often divert a teacher's attention from whether or the degree to which the 'tool' has 'built' lasting musical learning. The lesson may seem go smoothly, as planned, but such 'delivery' can unfortunately lead to the misimpression that it was effective in promoting significant and lasting musical learning. The medium is thus routinely mistaken for the message.

Regarding such teaching methods (didactics) as 'how to' prescriptions, "what works" and "best practices" recipes leads to the many criticisms of the *factory model* of schooling. As a cartoon amusingly pointed out, if everyone is following "best practices," they must all be, by definition, mediocre (i.e., average, unexceptional, second rate, ordinary). In those all too common (and rightly criticized) models, students are regarded as uniform products to be produced on an assembly line through uniform methods according to uniform standards of 'quality control'. Such "methodolatry" is properly avoided in praxially inspired music education, where, instead, only musical results are at focus.*

'Good methods', then, are those that (a) predictably produce positive results for students' present and predicted musicking abilities and dispositions (b) under the specific teaching and learning conditions that prevail. Thus, the 'goodness' of a teaching "strategy" (an interesting war-based term of educational jargon) cannot be pronounced in *advance*. Successful pedagogies and *learning materials* (e.g., scores, concert programs, classroom "song series," "methods series" for beginning instrumental students, teaching software) are qualified only by having produced good (i.e., productive, pragmatic, and perpetually relevant) results for students.

As praxis (rather than as techne or methodolatry), teaching thus approximates the *professional praxis* of, for example, doctors, lawyers, therapists, clergy, social workers, and the other helping professions. The 'standards' of such helping professions are not *standard* (i.e., uniform or standardized).† Even "evidence-based" medicine based on scientific studies involves praxis that informs decision making and is not 'delivered' formulaically.

Instead, and importantly, the 'standards' of the helping professions are ethical *standards of care*. They amount to an *ethical* responsibility that assesses successful praxis in terms of beneficial results for clients—in our case, clear benefits for our students. Teachers in all subjects should consider their planning deliberations, judgments, and pedagogies along the lines of, say, various medical professions, where failure to achieve pragmatic results is not simply a pragmatic dysfunction (in original Greek terms, dyspraxis); over time, it amounts to *mal-praxis* (i.e., professional malpractice).*† Clients and patients can get worse, even die. That image can be useful for teachers faced with musically 'sick' students where 'dying' means quitting.†

For **students**, praxial knowledge that accumulates through progressive use in one or more musical praxis leads to effective *independent musicianship*.† This involves all attitudes, dispositions, and skills that enable a student, especially later as an adult, to be musically active and productive to a degree that is personally rewarding without reliance on a teacher or other authorities. It can also include, for example, the ability to find scores, use the Internet or library for information and resources, find and learn to use fingering charts and tablature, transpose, know appropriate conventions of interactive behavior for a musical praxis, consult social media on the Internet that involve relevant musicking, and so on.

In a praxial context, knowing how to practice† is perhaps the most central kind of praxial knowledge serving musical independence. Yet, this praxial knowledge is rarely addressed by teachers. Instead of just assigning practice time, teachers should make monitoring and improving a student's practicing habits part of every lesson. Practicing, in a praxial context, is a matter not of *quantity* of time spent but of the *quality* of the results.† "Less is best when done well" (or "less is more") is a motto to keep in mind in working with children and teens whose time demands are challenged by a wide variety of competing interests that they willingly 'practice' or engage in. Youth are guaranteed to gravitate to what they think is "worth-while" (i.e., "good time"). And practicing music too often suffers from competing interests that are seen as more worth-while.

Effective musical independence facilitates the lifelong musicking of seriously committed amateurs.* As the term "amateur" indicates, amateurs are "lovers" (*amat* is Latin for "love"). Teaching that promotes "amateuring" (a verb form, like "musicking) and amateur dispositions seeks to increase musical choices—in comparison to the fewer choices students had when starting their school studies or at the beginning of a particular school year, term, or class. Their knowledge and musicianship skills are developed, then, in accordance with (or as a result of) engaging with musicking via in-school models or exemplars of actual adult musical praxis.† Such initiations into praxis serve at least as the entry level for amateur and everyday musicking. Just as a baby's crawling leads to lurching around unsteadily, then to more stable walking, then to (too much) running around, so the entry level of musicking progresses over time to an ever-more functional status.

All such 'real-life' musical practices that are included in school curriculums can serve as the foundation for the lifelong pursuit of specialized or more expert knowledge and ability. For example, learning a single chord on the guitar progresses to three-chord blues as an entry-level stage for expanding to a richer range of chords, to jazz, to improvisation, to composition, and so on. In such a progression, the student's intentionality determines what is next to be accomplished. Or, having reached a certain stage of expertise, an amateur may rest content with performing familiar literature and adding new literature involving the same level of skills.

In curriculum theory, the use of *life-based models for school curriculum* has been called "Action Learning." And we now can turn attention to curricular matters.

. . .

The term "curriculum" comes from the Latin for "a course run" (i.e., a sequence of 'content', skills, and learning experiences). Thus, such a "course run" can take one of three possible forms.

Some teachers have a written curriculum document (often at the insistence of principals). Such "planned curriculums" are typically found, if they exist at all, on dusty shelves in the music room or suite and, as many student teachers learn, are rarely, if ever, consulted by their "master teacher" (which is why they are dusty).

Second, there is what can be called the "instructed" curriculum. This kind of curriculum involves whatever knowledge and skills are *actually addressed* in lessons and rehearsals during the "course [of studies] run" with students. For this curriculum, however, what is included in *instruction* is not necessarily *learned* by students. This sense of 'delivered' instruction often has no relationship to any written document or long-term planning, and it typically consists only of whatever 'bus route' teaching has become habitual for the teacher. 'Delivery-methods' typically involve such "activities" and "experiences."

The third kind of curriculum is an "action" curriculum. This entails what the students *actually learn* in the "course run" that they can act upon and with musically. It might also be considered a "praxial" curriculum. It consists of what students learn effectively enough to put into praxis in their musical lives. This model is explained more fully in the focus of the next chapter, which focuses on Action Learning as a praxial conception of curriculum.†

From a praxial perspective, then, the third kind of curriculum is what should be at stake. It is not concerned with "benchmarks," any alliance to "Common Core" ideology, or "national standards." These abstractions sound politically correct on paper but too often don't amount to *musical* learning that is effective and lasting. In addition, the first and foremost intention of such praxial planning is *music*, not a matter of lip service to criteria that, however ideologically popular with politicians and some members of the public, do not lead to musicianship skills and dispositions of much pragmatic or lasting merit.

The attempts of music educators to 'fit' into or to 'go along' with the straitjacket of such ideologies are misplaced. Resistance, instead, implies the need to create alternative values and criteria. Thus, *after* an effective praxial curriculum of *music* is devised, *then*, if (additionally) needed, it can be *rationalized* as being in line with such politically motivated ideologies (e.g., that listening lessons promote language arts or that rhythmic reading practices math). The content of the curriculum, therefore, is *musical* and the other benefits (usually reading and math) are side effects, not primary results.

Even in the milieu of local politics (another evidence of the social concerns of schooling and of the need for music education to be functionally useful in life), music teachers will best serve their students by following a praxis-based curriculum that is *locally notable* for the enthusiasm and musical achievements of students and for contributions to community musicking. Models do exist that clearly demonstrate the praxial values and persuasion detailed here (more follows later). Despite all the political and social controversy over student testing as evidence of a teacher's contribution to students and society, a praxial curriculum based in Action Learning and the action ideal† of "breaking 100 in music"† can in fact produce more relevant, reality-based evidence and 'testing' of students and of local curriculum.

One thing is for sure: Parents respond to their children's enthusiasm for music not just as reflecting the personality and charisma of a teacher but in terms of the discernible and substantial effects of music education on their children's lives. A praxial curriculum will, first of all, build on the natural attraction of music for students. Second, this will appeal to parents and the rest of the community in ways and to a degree that confirms both a praxial focus for musicking and community support for the values of school music that students convey to their parents.

A rural school in western New York gives ample and clear evidence of this by virtue of the recognition given to praxial music teacher Kent Knappenberger and his Action Learning curriculum, which was so notable and deserving of attention that he was the first-ever winner, in 2014, of the Music Educator Award presented by The Recording Academy and the GRAMMY Foundation. Not only has the curriculum attracted local attention; it has attracted national attention. *Check it out.**

Related Readings

C.D.C. Reeve. *Aristotle on Practical Wisdom: Nicomachean Ethics VI.* Cambridge, MA: Harvard University Press, 2013.
A detailed analysis of the ethos of phronesis. See pp. 183–184 for the quotation from Aristotle.

Thomas A. Regelski. "Music and Music Education—Theory and Praxis for 'Making a Difference'." *Educational Philosophy and Theory* 37(1) (January 2005): 7–27. Special journal issue republished as *Music Education for the New Millennium: Theory and Practice Futures for Music Teaching and Learning.* Oxford: Blackwell, 2005; same pagination.
Support from pragmatism for praxial music education.

Thomas A. Regelski. "Music Education: What Is the 'Value Added' for Self and Society?" In B. Stålhammar, ed., *Music and Human Beings*. Örebro, Sweden: University of Örebro, 2006; 71–90.
A 'valued added' examination of music education as praxis.

Nicholas Cook. "Music as Performance." In M. Clayton, T. Herbert, and R. Middleton, eds., *The Cultural Study of Music: A Critical Introduction*. London: Routledge, 2003; 204–214.
A performative philosophy of music: performance as "the music," not the score!

John Searle. *Intentionality*. Cambridge: Cambridge University Press, 1983.
On the 'aboutness' of intentionality in comparison to mere 'activity'.

Thomas A. Regelski. *Teaching General Music in Grades 4–8*. New York: Oxford University Press, 2004.
On teaching "tween-agers," pp. 29–51 (also relevant for instrumental teachers).

Ellen Dissanayake. *Art and Intimacy*. Seattle: University of Washington Press, 2012.
A study from cultural anthropology on the 'loving' relation people have to art and art's role in loving human relationships.

Martin Stokes, ed. *Ethnicity, Identity and Music: The Musical Construction of Place*. Oxford: Berg 1997.

"Knowing Practice." Special issue of *Pedagogy, Culture and Society* 13(3) (2005).
Seven articles on praxial knowledge.

Pentti Määttänen. "Meaning as Use: Peirce and Wittgenstein." In F. Stadler and M. Stoltzner, eds., *Time and History*, vol. 13. Kirchberm am Wechsel: Austrian Ludwig Wittgenstein Society, 2005; 171–172.
The pragmatic philosophy of meaning as use: the meaning of "hat" is what you 'do' with it.

Wayne C. Booth. *For the Love of It: Amateuring and Its Rivals*. Chicago: University of Chicago Press, 1999.
Barenboim quotation, p. 88. This book is an excellent account of dedicated amateurs of string chamber music. It also contains ample evidence of how poor teaching turns off students.

Thomas A. Regelski. "On 'Methodolatry' and Music Teaching as Critical and Reflective Praxis." *Philosophy of Music Education Review* 10(2) (Fall 2002): 102–124.
On the perils of 'delivery methods'.

Thomas De Baets and Thade Buchborn, eds. *European Perspectives on Music Education 3: The Reflective Music Teacher*. Innsbruck, Austria: Esslinger/Helbling, 2014.
Articles on reflective praxis in music education by European researchers.

Thomas A. Regelski. "Reflective Music Education as a Helping Profession." In T. De Baets and T. Buchborn, eds., *European Perspectives on Music Education 3: The Reflective Music Teacher*. Innsbruck, Austria: Esslinger/Helbling, 2014.

Thomas A. Regelski. "The Good Life of Teaching or the Life of Good Teaching?" *Action, Criticism, and Theory for Music Education* 11(2): 42–78; http://act.mayday group.org/articles/Regelski11_2.pdf (accessed May 15, 2015).
A philosophical study of ethics and malpractice in music education.

David Carr. *Professionalism and Ethics in Teaching*. New York: Routledge, 2000.

Sarah V. Mackenzie and G. Calfin Mackenzie. *Now What? Confronting and Resolving Ethical Questions: A Handbook for Teachers.* Thousand Oaks, CA: Corwin/SAGE, 2010.

Thomas A. Regelski. "Amateuring in Music and Its Rivals." *Action, Criticism, and Theory for Music Education* 6(3) (2007): 22–50; http://act.maydaygroup.org/articles/Regelski6_3.pdf (accessed May 15, 2015).
An application of Booth (cited earlier) to music education.

Thomas A. Regelski. *Teaching General Music in Grades 4–8.* New York: Oxford University Press, 2004.
Offers a model of an actual, written Action Learning and praxis-based curriculum, pp. 257–265; also see the index under "Curriculum" for more details about curriculum theory in music education.

On the 2014 Grammy-winning praxial curriculum of Kent Knappenberger (he also won a local competition for the best beard), see: http://www.grammy.com/news/kent-knappenberger-the-grammycom-interview (accessed May 15, 2015).
And (in this order):

https://www.youtube.com/watch?v=XaPDBRUUJs0
https://www.youtube.com/watch?v=WrOPAmJwmYU
https://www.youtube.com/watch?v=cmQ8k_73HmM
https://www.youtube.com/watch?v=1bvdAyvlScg

Note: Several of these have "up next" continuations that give further details (accessed April 29, 2015):

Performances of The McClurg Street String Band (includes some community members). This ensemble is generated entirely from middle and high school general music classes:

https://www.youtube.com/watch?v=0307zoqLCGQ;
https://www.youtube.com/watch?v=hLBk-1VtxJ8;
https://www.youtube.com/watch?v=QnYOQd2Ssbk;
https://www.youtube.com/watch?v=QQct_M3qYuY;

(accessed May 1, 2015).

For more details, Google "Kent Knappenberger." To inquire about his curriculum, readers may contact him at kknappennberger@WACS2.wnyric.org or elevation@gmail.com ("Elevation" is his favorite cow!).

7

ACTION LEARNING AND "BREAKING 100 IN MUSIC"

By treating all music students as musical practitioners, and by teaching all students how to find and solve musical problems in 'conversation' with specific musical praxes, music educators situate students' musical thinking and knowing. In doing so, the various kinds of knowing involved in musical understanding develop and cohere.

. . .

One of the most important educational features of the curriculum-as-practicum is that it contextualizes or situates learning. When teachers place productive musical actions at the center of the music curriculum, students experience the practicality of several related forms of music knowing immediately and regularly. They witness the reasons underlying musical procedures, practices, and concepts and grasp these reasons concretely.

David J. Elliott and Marissa Silverman*

Curriculum theory is rarely addressed in music education. One reason seems to be that 'delivery-methods," 'what works', "best practices," and the like are mistakenly taken to be curriculum. 'Delivering' a lesson according to a standard methodology is taken to be the curriculum. Using such a method or 'guaranteed' practice as the basis for a lesson, then, ends up 'delivering' the method but not necessarily any lasting musical learning or skill.

Such lessons typically end up being isolated or free-standing "activities" that are rationalized as being for the purpose of "experiencing" concepts: for example, the many lessons designed to teach the concept of "high and low." Though supposedly the lesson is about melodic pitch, students can be confused about loud and quiet music: Mom says, "Turn the music down; it's up too high." And, in any case, the concept is seen in action in successful music reading, which too often is not the result of such lessons.

However, curriculum for the most part is less concerned with the 'how' of teaching (the 'delivery') than with the 'what' is to be included in instruction and 'why' (capital "P") and with related social issues, problems, and challenges.*

The 'how' should follow from the 'what' and 'why' deliberations. Lessons (or rehearsals), then, that are focused on musicianship skills (general or specific)† should feature the praxial conditions to which such skills are applicative. And they should be judged by the conditions of authentic praxis: Has the 'how' of teaching promoted the 'what' and 'why' of learning? Where it hasn't, the 'hows' (the 'tools') need rethinking.

Teachers following an agreed-upon curriculum may well differ in the details of their pedagogy, just as carpenters following a blueprint may select and use different tools to accomplish the same ends. The criterion at stake, then, is what is 'built' according to some sense of a curricular blueprint. And, a succession of "activities," no matter how much fun or how smoothly 'delivered', does not necessarily add up to 'building' worthwhile musical learning. In fact, too often, such student-friendly lessons (and students often do respond well to the 'fun' of such activities) amount to no or scant learning of any long-term merit. In fact, few if any musical skills or useful knowledge typically end up being taught in such classrooms.

For all the lessons about "high and low" and "melody" and "rhythm" in elementary schools following the "activities approach" and endless 'delivery methods' predicated on "teaching concepts," too many students (in the United States, at least) cannot match pitch or read music (unless they also have studied an instrument)—the claimed purpose of such "concept" learning. (Estonian students, in comparison, read music well and freely. Thus, the country is very song-oriented, and the massive song festival there in 1988, attended by more than 300,000 people, a quarter of the population at that time, resulted in the "singing revolution" of the three Baltic countries seeking to be free of the Soviet Union. This is just more evidence of the social power of music!) And, as real evidence of the *lack* of *professional integrity*, Internet sites are full of lesson plans that are said to "work." Some teachers even buy and sell their lesson plans on line. This practice obviously lends itself to the critique of 'cookie-cutter' teaching and shows no evidence at all of curricular direction or effectiveness!

Curriculum theory is no better in ensembles. There, the curriculum appears to amount only to x-years of literature 'covered' in presenting x-number of concerts for x-years that students are members (maybe up to eight years total, but not all students stay members that long). Any specific attempt to address musicianship skills and musical independence are often altogether lacking. Too often, the director makes all the musical decisions and rarely even informs the group of the musical reasoning that is usually at stake (Why not breathe there? Just don't breathe there!).

The uncritical and unsubstantiated assumption is that learning and playing the chosen literature (automatically) develop musicianship and, as criticized in Part One, are rationalized as being (automatically) aesthetic and therefore (still automatically) are educational and (yes, automatically) valuable. No other steps or curricular plans are needed beyond selecting a year's worth of literature for concerts and rehearsing it for performance. Just performing the literature in concert is assumed to be a meaningful music education (at least according to the aesthetic ideology).

The idea of studying music that will not be heard in concert but that *educationally* promotes musicianship skills of certain kinds is considered altogether aberrant (or abhorrent). Instead, directors select music on the basis of students' likes (e.g., arrangements from the latest Disney movies for younger ensembles). Or they select compositions on the basis of interesting concert programing—meaning that the interests of the audience determine 'curriculum', not whether the music studied and performed progressively advances general or specific musicianship skills that can support a lifetime of performing. And just producing what seems (more to the director, often, than to the audience who are there to see their children perform) to be a competent performance is assumed to have been aesthetic and to have taught "music." In this extreme version of the aesthetic ideology, "music" is having reproduced the selected scores, and the assumption (easily tested, though no one is interested in doing this) is that students have learned musicianship skills that are worthy of their time and the school's expense.

Asking an ensemble director, then, about curriculum typically results only in mention of the "program" and its aspirations—usually citing "high standards" and the numbers of students in the "program."† Thus, the topic of *curriculum,* as such, typically goes altogether unaddressed in music education conducting methods courses and, of course, in 'delivery-methods' and "activities approach" courses. Just as in conducting courses where students perfect "how" to 'deliver' the next concert, so do general music classes often 'deliver' a "program" of music activities that are not progressively structured to produce even the 'performance' of important musicianship skills. Nebulous reference to our "program" also hides the fact that a "program" of studies, by definition, indicates a planned, organized, and progressive sequence that aims to be accountable for significant learning.

In a subject such as language arts, the reading "program" is understood to refer to such a calculated *progression* of lessons and related instructional materials, and not just to a list of stories and books ("experiences") to be read. And, in the current climate of high-stakes testing, language arts teachers are held accountable. (What if general music teachers had to be accountable for the music reading and pitch matching competencies of, say, sixth-grade students—after seven years of rote songs and music reading "activities" and "experiences"?) Thus, reading teachers tend to be very pragmatic and praxially oriented.

In contrast, attempts to teach "music reading" in classroom music often fail (unless classroom instruments are the basis for instruction, thus not compounding the problems many students have in combining *pitch matching* with *vocal music reading*).* And even where music reading *is* accomplished, mainly in instrumental ensembles (because not enough choral teachers make teaching music reading a primary curricular goal), the easy assumption is made that teaching music reading—the decoding of musical notation—is "teaching music."

This equation of "music" with "notation" is often assumed by students as an effect of the "hidden curriculum."† In the United States, a student will say, "I left my *music* at home," whereas in many parts of Europe the same excuse will be expressed as "I left my *notes* at home." This confusion of "music" with "notation" is,† of course, attributable to the focus of the aesthetic ideology on 'works' as printed music. And what passes for 'curriculum' that is not much more than the selection of concert repertory falls dutifully in line with the aesthetic ideology. 'Works' are performed in concert and, thus, as the theory goes, "music" has been learned to the (automatic) benefits of students.

Curriculum theory can get into a host of philosophical, social, and pedagogical tensions among teachers (of any subject). This concluding chapter, however, offers what is hoped to be a clear and straightforward approach to curriculum. The answer to "what" to teach is *music*. The answer to 'why' teach music is its importance for sociality and personhood. The answer to 'how' to teach is through practicums of relevant *musicking*. The answer to assessment and accountability of the curriculum or "program" is the *evidence* of pragmatic musicianship skills in one or more music praxis. The answer to "what is your philosophy of music education" is "to involve students in musicking in ways and to a degree that serves their musical needs throughout life."

As with any "action ideal" (such as 'good health,' 'good parent,' or 'good friend'), there is no final, once-and-for all successful stage ever reached.† Yet, as with these examples, action ideals are needed to guide us toward a better life result—or teaching results—than would otherwise be the case. In essence, then, curriculum should be clear as to the tangible action ideals for musicking that it seeks.

. . .

Action Learning

Action Learning is a curriculum model that brings examples of authentic exemplars of 'real life' into the classroom in preparing students for life outside and after graduation from school.* Perhaps its most currently seen form is "language immersion." In such classes, the praxis of a foreign language is learned by involvement in a classroom-created micro-society of the targeted language group and culture. Thus, the only language spoken and read in the classroom is the target language. Action Learning is also found in physical education classes that go beyond just providing an exercise break or outlet from deskbound classes. Such physical education classes (not just "activities" that let off steam) provide instruction that aims at getting students involved in sports and healthy physical activities that they can and will be more inclined to pursue outside and after graduation from school—especially individual sports (e.g., archery, swimming, gymnastics) and small-group sports (e.g., tennis, handball) that can more easily be fit into the lives of busy adults than can team sports. Biology classes that study the environment and other real-life applications of biology in daily living are also examples of Action Learning. It is likewise found in chemistry classes that focus on chemicals in the home and the chemistry of daily life and the environment. And praxially oriented math pedagogies focus on solving real-world problems, rather than on "pure" (abstract) mathematics.

Action Learning for music education similarly involves bringing likely models of *authentic musicking* from the music world outside school into the classroom with the intention of preparing students to be more disposed and better able to enrich their musical lives outside school and as adults. (Ever want to play dulcimer, penny whistle, mandolin, or Celtic harp? Access the video links at the end of Chapter 6 to see students who thoroughly enjoy such instruments!)† It focuses, first of all, on musicking that is already popular or accessible in a community, society, region, or locality.

It also identifies examples of musical praxis that may not be currently in vogue—practices that could easily become more accessible, popular, and rewarding if advanced by school music curriculums, such as more and more musically significant or rewarding use of music apps and composition software; or local chamber music groups (pursing all kinds of musics: rock, jazz, ethnic, folk, "garage bands," and vocal groups but also participating in the standard repertory of 'classical' music, such as duets and trios) that meet regularly for their own participatory musical interests. It especially fosters musical pursuits that students, later in life as adults, can most easily integrate into their busy work, family, and social lives: for example, bell choirs for church; various musical hobbies, such as use of composition software; or string duos and trios in schools too small to have an orchestra. That potential string students are denied this opportunity is an indictment of the status quo emphasis on only large ensembles. What about the students, for whatever reason (a model in the family and thus a violin in the closet)? Why are they ignored? This important criterion helps ensure that a musical practice will continue to be appreciated throughout life. (Do adult and senior citizen groups exist in the community? If not, why not?)

Large performance groups can be at something of a disadvantage in this regard; scheduling ensemble rehearsals at convenient times for substantial numbers of busy adults (and interested students) is difficult. This may be why so few community groups exist. Such scheduling problems can eliminate those whose work and family schedules cannot be adapted to those of the rest of the group. Thus, their own practicing and performing are often sacrificed.

Solo performance and chamber groups, in a variety of musical genres, have the most likely chance of being worked into a busy adult life. Take, for example, the three mothers—a Juilliard graduate, a music teacher, and a flute-playing liberal arts graduate—who met twice a week to play all the literature they could find in a local university library for flute, piano, and oboe while their infants slept in the bedroom (or enjoyed the music, quietly or not). Then they started to transpose other music for their 'ensemble'. Or consider the two doctors, a lawyer and a public school English teacher, who got together regularly to sing barbershop music; or former U.S. Secretary of State Condoleezza Rice, an accomplished pianist, who gets together frequently with lawyer friends (all conservatory trained) to play chamber music (see her Wikipedia page).

In today's technological world, also beneficial are musical interests centering on the computer, such as composition software, and especially the apps for smartphones and tablets. For example, a MIDI instrument can be played without disturbing the neighbors (remember Kant's objection to the loud singing of his Lutheran neighbors).† Otherwise, acoustic instruments too often go into the closet upon graduation and people stop playing or practicing at home. And MIDI instruments offer a host of possibilities beyond just playing "the notes," such as creating innovative arrangements (e.g., adding a rhythm track), modifying and experimenting with timbres, and accommodating other interests.

Electronic keyboards and guitars can be enjoyed at home alone (and, if needed, with earphones). And because the music they offer is complete (not just a solo line), it is therefore more musically rewarding in itself. Many who have learned to play band or orchestra instruments, however, rarely (if ever) have had the pleasures of playing with accompaniment. MIDI accompaniment software that 'follows' a soloist* solves that problem if the teacher cannot provide an accompaniment—or can't arrange for an accompaniment by a local piano student, thus modeling for both students further possibilities for musicking. (A school music website can facilitate such kinds of local musicking by students and adults. A student who has studied piano and who has no dream of a concert career can thus be productive locally with instrumental soloists and other chamber musics.) Students whose study includes such holistic enhancements are simply more likely to want to and be able to continue to play. Other skills, such as the ability to do basic transposition typical for an instrument, can promote performing with like-minded others. The possibilities are limitless, yet the steady diet of most school music 'programs' amounts to not much more than band, chorus, and orchestra for three concerts a year.

One actual example of simply taught praxis was the two fathers-in-law (one from Germany, the other from Italy), a saxophonist and a trumpet player, who wanted to know how to learn to play lead sheets of 'popular' songs (and, no doubt, familiar opera tunes) in the same key. This was easily taught to them, but the praxial aspects of their *wanting* to do this as part of the 'good life' should not be ignored.

And the range of musical interests that are addressed by the exponential growth of musical games should not be dismissed or overlooked. Many students who enjoy GuitarHero® become motivated to study guitar. Explorations made possible by composition software and apps open a realm of possibilities that can lead to ever more and more sophisticated musical accomplishments. 'Group composition', where musical ideas are shared, explored, and shaped collectively through social media, can add an entirely new communal dimension to the practice of composition, just as 'studio composition' did generations ago and continues to do today. (Music education students in the celebrated Sibelius Academy in Finland take a one-year course in studio musicking. The class is divided into 'combos' of four or five students, and each student 'leads' the organization of a composition. For each of the performances, each student plays a different instrument, those of others in the group. How typical is that elsewhere?)

Far too often such musicking is ignored when schools favor large ensembles to the exclusion of almost everything else. Predictable problems faced by large ensembles include, for example, rehearsing only for the next concert and students practicing an isolated part that is not, at the time it is being practiced at home (*if* it is practiced at home), holistically (musically) satisfying. Such a 'curriculum' thus amounts only to a student's school exposure to so many years of concert literature, not to the systematic learning of independent musicianship skills (general or specific)† and other praxial knowledge and dispositions that can lead to a lifetime of personal musicking. Also, the difficulties of diagnosing, monitoring, and guiding the musicianship skills of *individual* students in large groups typically results in their lack of competence in such useful knowledge and skills. From the "competency-based education" curriculums of the 1980s we might learn the old-fashioned curricular goal of developing actual musical competency.

Note, again, that when all musical decisions are made by the ensemble director (which is unfortunately too typical), the advancement of the ability for *independent* musical judgments by students is sacrificed.† And, finally, there's the problem of directors who 'perform' a school ensemble as though the students were merely organ pipes that are used exhibit the teacher's musical abilities. Such performances can appear to be musically impressive but unfortunately can be attained too often without benefitting students individually in musical ways that last beyond the pleasures of the moment or the last concert.

Action Learning, in contrast, is centrally concerned with importing real-life musicking into the school curriculum in ways and to a degree that are as musically *authentic* as possible—given the limitations of formal schooling. Sweden's curricular guideline of "from life into school," mentioned earlier,† has an Action Learning focus. In music education, recently there has been new theorizing about "informal" learning pedagogies and didactics in schools that parallel the informal 'studio composition' processes by which rock, jazz, ethnic, and folk music musicians compose, learn, practice, and improve as a *community of praxis*† (also known, in institutional and corporate theory, as a "learning organization").* And more and more notice is being taken of the praxis of participatory musics (e.g., gospel and church choirs, steel pan drums, handbell choirs, app ensembles).

In comparison to the typical presentational performances of ensembles,† where the ensemble prepares music to be listened to by parents and friends who do not otherwise participate in the musicking, with participatory performance all present are participants (or potential participants) at some level (according to skill differences, interests, and so on). Consider, for example, "sing-alongs" ("synchronous chorusing") such as caroling, where musicking becomes a keen source of the action of "performing sociality."* Drumming circles are a good example, but so are the "Sacred Harp" praxis and similar shape-note traditions of choral singing; conferences where amateurs get together simply to play chamber music with one another;* and the musicking of Appalachian, Irish, and British folk music and dance traditions.* "Garage bands" (and barbershop or vocal jazz groups) that never make it out of the garage also qualify.

An Action Learning curriculum in effect takes the form of a *practicum*. In effect, it is an *apprenticeship* in a *musicianship laboratory* (the classroom or ensemble) that *systematically* develops musicking through Action Learning.* It is *not* an introduction to music as a discipline. Nor does it regard students as empty mind (*tabula rasa*) that need to be filled with background information or preliminary skills *before* they can become musically active in valid ways.† These skills are promoted by and through mindful musical action. As seen earlier, we learn and improve our concept of "balance" by walking, riding a bicycle, and skiing. Again, concepts—as verbal abstractions or terms—arise from actions and then come into play only to the degree that words are useful.†

To the earlier mentioned premise of the Swedish curricular guidelines of "from life into school,"† Action Learning adds the next logical step of "and back into life." The point is not just to make school-based music learning relevant and more useful. The point is to *encourage* its use, to *maximize* what psychologists of education call "transfer of learning" from school into real-life musical practices. Successful teaching, then, is seen in the *lasting* musical difference made in the musical dispositions and thus the lives of students as a result of their school music studies. And it is seen in the collective effect of such a value-added concept to the musical vitality of society and its many musical subcultures—all of them.*

Again, to be successful in such ways, the "action" in Action Learning is not to be equated simply with mere "activity." With the so-called *activities approach* students are simply led to "experience" (as the jargon goes) so-called music 'concepts' via 'fun activities', but they are not mindfully 'trying to' or intending to learn for personal and lifelong *musical* purposes.† Action Learning enhances the motivation for a lasting music learning because students are aware of the relevance of their school music studies to their out-of-school and after-graduation musical lives and are not just taking part or 'going along' for momentary interests or short-term pleasures. "Why do we have to study this?" is a question that should rarely arise; the relevance of study, beyond its immediate potential for pleasure, is perfectly obvious. (A player to the basketball coach: "Why do we have to practice shooting foul shots? Or dribbling?") "Off-task" misbehavior is remedied with a simple reminder of the musical goals at hand.

With a curriculum based on the aesthetic theory of art and music, the intangible goal of promoting and advancing something called "aesthetic responsiveness" is said to be the value at stake. However, and to the contrary, progress and achievement from Action Learning are easily observed and assessed in terms of tangible musical growth and according to the musical choices students make—as students and later as adults. *Authentic assessment* is the primary vehicle for evaluating both teaching and learning: The very same authentic musical practices that are the sources and goals of student's musical learning are the means of evaluating success and progress.†

"Breaking 100 in Music"

As foretold many pages ago in the Introduction, the *action ideal*† of music education as praxis is to make a difference in what music education in schools has to offer beside the next concert or classroom activity. How many times can you sing catchy tunes with students in music classes to no growth of musicianship skills? How many listening lessons or music reading "activities" have no lasting musical impact on listening choices and habits? How many rehearsals of performances that will be heard only in one-time concerts will add up to a music *education* by any pragmatic criteria?

Think about it: What *difference* does most of music education as currently practiced make in the lives of students, not to mention in their musical lives as adults?† How many colleagues who were in your high school ensembles are musically engaged today in ways that can be credited to the experience of what often turns out to be a high school *social* activity that doesn't outlast the school years? And what of the many students who quit ensembles after elementary and middle school? How have they profited musically? What does their rejection signify about the failure to meet their musical needs and why their initial enthusiasm waned? And what alternatives might have sustained their interests?†

In sharp contrast, the motto of what has been called "breaking 100 in music" is the praxial goal of Action Learning.* Consumer studies of golfers show that they are more inclined to mindful and purpose-driven practice and serious application as they improve their game. Thus, once they start to "break 100"— that is, when they regularly start to score *under* 100 for eighteen holes—they are more motivated and, importantly, spend more money in pursuit of the sport ("golfing widows" beware!). In the opposite direction, when beginners start to score *over* 100 in bowling, they join leagues, get uniforms, buy their equipment instead of renting it, and regularly practice their skills. (Whether or not such research was well done, the advertising premise seems solid.)

In music, however, there are no such numerical thresholds. Instead, "breaking 100" is the *psychological* "tipping point" at which a student becomes *serious* about and committed to pursuing a particular musical praxis because of the musical, social, and personal pleasures it offers. The student thus practices more, collects and listens to recordings, attends concerts, shares interests with like-minded others, and seeks not just to "find time" for musicking but "makes time" for it. Music thus becomes part of the student's Self, just as serious amateur golfers identify with their sport. A stone memorial on the third hole of my favorite golf course has a plaque with the name of a deceased golfing buddy who is identified as a "real golfer." That obviously doesn't mean a "professional" golfer but illustrates the *serious amateur* dedication involved. What does it take to be a "real musician," in the same sense? Are those who are professionally trained and perform for money the only "real musicians"? Or can serious amateurs in their diverse—and more numerous—ways be "real musicians"?

The answer is that a life without regularly 'doing' music in personally rewarding ways—for pay or not—becomes unimaginable to those who have experienced "breaking 100 in music." When and how have readers "broken 100 in music"? That question from "symbolic interactionism," a sociological theory about socially constructed meaning, might help music teachers to recall the conditions that led to their own commitment to music—as long as they, as teachers, don't try to simply imitate those musical initiating interests with their own students ("I am a music teacher due to the competition with my peers that led me to want to be the best of them, to get first-chair honors and do all the important solos. Therefore, I will create the same conditions that cause my students to excel over others."). The conditions of "breaking 100" need to be 'found' by students, not 'programmed' into them. And they are 'found' only by treating students, of whatever age, as practitioners of a musical praxis.

Many people achieve the "breaking 100" state of mind and commitment without direct help or support from school music or private teachers. For example, self-taught musicians are more likely to continue to practice and perform than those who study with a teacher. When lessons cease, those who have studied with a teacher no longer have any motivation or reason to practice. The next lesson had been their extrinsic musical goal, not the musical pleasures of playing better.

The Internet, therefore, is filled with self-help sites of all kinds devoted to various forms of musicking not often addressed by school music. However, with direct help and a curricular focus in school (including learning how to access the Internet, use apps, locate resources in libraries, transpose, and so on), far more people could be enjoying the benefits of "breaking 100 in music." They would be more able and more inclined to include music in their lives in significant ways, to a more significant degree, or with greater rewards and pleasures.

This result would minimize the legitimation crisis† faced by school music teachers and reduce the ever-pressing need for advocacy.† The value of music education would be perfectly evident from the robustness of musicking in the community and society that could be honestly attributed to school music. How much of such considerable music activity in modern life is the direct result of music education? Most, it seems, has little or no relation to school music or private music lessons. Musicking is happening outside of schools, and teachers are 'missing the boat' as far as what it has to offer to students and the community.

This was decidedly the result with the praxial teaching and curriculum that led to the success of the Grammy Award–winning teacher mentioned at the end of Chapter 6. Following word for word his well-considered explanations and observing example after example of enthusiastic students engaged in competent musicking give us pragmatic evidence of the success of that praxial and Action Learning curriculum in that community, with that teacher.

So, when music is considered as praxis, it is valued not just for its hedonistic appeal but as a 'doing' that is creative of Self, of society, and of the various subcultures that make up any society. When music is regarded as praxis, it loses none of its nobility or profundity. In fact, its ever-present *abundance* demonstrates its value to the life well lived, in our case, lived in part—but in significant ways—through music. Consequently, the idea that "music is basic" in schooling becomes an empirical fact and not an empty advocacy cliché.†
Considered as and for praxis, then, music education becomes valued for the notable contributions it makes to the vitality of the music world outside the school, especially in the local community. (Note, in the videos cited at the end of Chapter 6, the relevance of school bell choirs to local churches. Indeed, the teacher in question first "broke 100" in a church bell choir and started to compose and arrange for it as a youngster.)

Consequentially, then, music *education* conducted as praxis promotes *music* as praxis and, correspondingly, is also a form of *community music* education.*
It promotes making the kind of significant difference in the musical lives of students, the community, and society that demonstrates that music truly *is* basic—basic to education, basic to society, and especially basic to the life well lived. It demonstrates this by making a pragmatic difference that eliminates any question about the relevance of music education and thus avoids the need for the 'selling' efforts of advocacy. (The school in question in the videos has only seven hundred students at this writing, and yet the community supports four music teachers! That is very rare!)

Music Teaching as and for Praxis

Music teaching as praxis and for "breaking 100," then, is the primary goal of an Action Learning curriculum. It exists to get more people 'into action' musically by developing skills they otherwise would not have or use—at all, as well, as often, or as meaningfully. It formally expands the musical options and abilities of those who come to school with existing musical interests from the family, community, or commercial music or who are already musically active in some way (often in church as a typical supporting musical community). And it increases the likelihood that students not only will gain new musical knowledge and advanced skill but also will acquire the disposition to *want* to put that skill into action in their lives more often or more significantly or more enthusiastically than would have otherwise been the case without formal music education.

Interestingly, such results are rather easily accomplished simply. The first step is to acknowledge that music is one of the most valuable of all forms of sociality in any society. The next step is to honor that value by including *authentic models of musicking* as the basis for curriculum, pedagogy, methods, teacher account- ability, and student assessment. So, the challenge is for school music to honor, not ignore (as aesthetic theories do), the central personal and sociocultural role of all major forms of musical praxis. Praxialism thus ignores the claims of the aesthetic hierarchy.† All musics have social values, or they wouldn't exist.

Instead, the goal of all curriculum and pedagogy should be to get music educa- tion and students 'into action' in ways that both reflect and advance music as an essential personal and sociocultural praxis. Music education *as* and *for praxis** builds on the attractive and appealing aisthesic qualities of music† by further- ing the actual musical pursuits that are the major means by which people—of all ages, in all countries, in all cultural, ethnic, and subcultures—can most fully maximize the benefits of music's contribution to a rich personal life and, in doing so, create an even richer music world to the advantage of all in society.

. . .

Change has always been a historical variable. But it is happening much more rapidly and often more dramatically in the contemporary world of expanded media, social connectivity, and globalization. And change in the music world is no less (and is perhaps even more) rapid and dramatic. Such musically chang- ing times* thus bring about a compelling interest in meeting the musical needs of today's world and those of tomorrow, as well. The aesthetic theory of art and music is an ideology rooted in eighteenth-century assumptions and values. Even many of its former believers have openly confessed doubts about its rel- evance for the modern world.*

It is also regularly challenged by contemporary musics (e.g., 'popular', twelve-tone serialism, aleatoric, and stochastic musics), the sociology and anthropology of music, ethnomusicology, cultural studies, multicultural/world musics, and more (e.g., harmonica and accordion praxialists; the accordion, in fact, is often a conservatory study in Europe). These developments thus strug- gle mightily to rationalize the usual aesthetic accounts of such divergent artis- tic activity, and they continue to ignore social and cultural accounts of music and its value for society. In fact, as an ideology, the aesthetic creed is more and more rebelled against by contemporary artists and musicians.† As a result, it is largely ignored by creative artists in today's world; only professional aestheti- cians engage with its various puzzles and conjectures. That may be a source of their living, but it regularly fails to account for music as a living social praxis.†

As the social and musical world changes, so does (or should) schooling.* Educational developments in many countries rush to keep up with social changes. In fact, various tensions over educational change demonstrate that schooling is very much a focal point of social conflict—all the more so when it becomes the center of antagonistic social, political, and economic ideologies.

Much, then, is changing music education and will continue to do so. Given the clearly social nature of both music and schooling, music educators will do well to reconsider their allegiance to the rationale of the traditional aesthetic ideology, especially in light of the legitimation crisis it has promoted.†

A praxial perspective for both music and teaching is rooted in social science scholarship, social theory and philosophy, and contemporary cultural studies (e.g., those cited in the related readings of each chapter). Its basic educational reliance on down-to-earth pragmatic musical results defeats the "it's nice if you can afford it," "icing on the cake" status of music education as a curricular "frill."† And it demonstrates how vital and important music is for Self (personhood) and society.

Interestingly, this new focus on music education as and for music praxis is something of a step *back* in history to a time when the social role and value of musical praxis were solidly established, only to be pushed aside by the aesthetic social fashion. Despite the claims of that vogue, music has always remained intensely social and a major vehicle for human sociality. Its contributions to life, then, are not those extolled by aesthetic speculations. Its social importance is as natural to and for human life as language is.† The time is long overdue, therefore, for a firm return to the praxial role and the many social benefits of music and, by taking music off its aesthetic pedestal, for returning it to its important status as significant part of our social nature.

In effect, then, music educators need to go "back to the future."* This *end*, then, is, one hopes, the *beginning* of a praxial 'turn' in music education philosophy. *Musica practica* and Action Learning, along with "breaking 100 in music," are the keys to rejuvenating music education from its aesthetics-based stagnation. Despite the changes it proposes to the status quo, it is truly *conservative*. It seeks to 'conserve' the sociality of music denied by the aesthetic ideology.

Related Readings

David J. Elliott and Marissa Silverman. *Music Matters: A Philosophy of Music Education*, 2nd ed. New York: Oxford University Press, 2015.
   For the epigrams to this chapter, see pp. 421, 425.

Kathleen Bennett deMarrais and Margaret D. LeCompete. *The Way Schools Work: A Sociological Analysis of Education*. London: Addison Wesley Longman, 1998.
   For a survey of curriculum theory in relation to the "social stratification of knowledge" (i.e., class conflicts), pp. 186–255.

Thomas A. Regelski. *Teaching General Music in Grades 4–8: A Musicianship Approach*. New York: Oxford University Press, 2004.
   On teaching singing via instruments for music reading and on 'recreational' instruments in the classroom, pp. 190–234.

Thomas A. Regelski. "Action Learning versus the Pied Piper Approach." *Music Educators Journal* 69(8) (April 1983): 55–57.

The "Pied Piper" approach refers to students subjected to the "activities approach" who merrily follow the Pied Piper "activities" teacher to a negative end of no lasting musical learning.

Thomas A. Regelski. "Action Learning." *Music Educators Journal* 69(6) (February 1983): 46–50.
An early proposal from thirty years ago.

Thomas A. Regelski. "Getting into Action for Middle School Music." *Canadian Music Educator* 28(2) (December 1986): 43–54.

Thomas A. Regelski. *Teaching General Music: Action Learning for Middle and Secondary Schools.* New York: Schirmer Books, 1981.

Thomas A. Regelski. "Music Education as and for Praxis: An Action Learning Model." In A. Liimets and M. Mäessalu, *Music Inside and Outside the School.* New York: Peter Lang, 2011.
Also contains a survey of European research in music education from the regional ISME/European Association for Music in School (EAS) (July 2009) at the Estonian Academy of Music and Theatre in Tallinn, Estonia.

For MIDI accompaniment software: http://www.smartmusic.com (accessed May 15, 2015).

Chris Argyris. *On Organizational Learning.* Cambridge: Blackwell, 1999.
On "learning organizations," a concept from the ethos of corporations and the military that has eluded the field of music education.

Lucy Green. *Music, Informal Learning and the School: A New Classroom Pedagogy.* Burlington, VT: Ashgate, 2008.
*Informal pedagogy that, as described (and without caution) **could** devolve into a 'formal' pedagogy. It seems restricted in its potential to other than 'classical' musics.*

Sidsel Karlsen and Lauri Vakeva, eds. *Corroborating Informal Learning Pedagogy.* Newcastle upon Tyne (UK): Cambridge Scholars Publishing, 2012.
A further examination and perhaps a more cautious approach by several scholars of informal learning in music education.

Wayne C. Booth. *For the Love of It: Amateuring and Its Rivals.* Chicago: University of Chicago Press, 1999.
An engaging read about amateurs who seek out others for the purposes of amateuring. Some important critiques of traditional pedagogy are expressed by players who 'survived' skill-drill and "no pain, not gain" pedagogy. Note: "Amateuring" is a verb (like "musicking").

Thomas Turino. *Music as Social Life: The Politics of Participation.* Chicago: University of Chicago Press, 2008.
An ethnomusicological study of presentational, participatory, and studio-recording praxis.

Thomas A. Regelski. *Teaching General Music in Grades 4–8: A Musicianship Approach.* Oxford University Press, 2004.
On Action Learning, pp. 14–29, 219–225, 235–226; on "breaking 100 in music," pp. 20–29.

Thomas A. Regelski. "Music Education: What Is the 'Value Added' for Self and Society?" In B. Stålhammar, ed., *Music and Human Beings.* Örebro, Sweden: University of Örebro, 2006; 71–90.
A study of a value-added philosophy of praxial music education.

113

International Journal of Community Music; http://www.intellectbooks.co.uk/journals/view-journal,id=149/ (accessed May 15, 2015).

Marie McCarthy, ed. *Music Education as Praxis*. College Park: University of Maryland, 1999.
A collection of articles from a MayDay Group colloquium on the topic.

Kurt Blaukopf. *Musical Life in a Changing Society: Aspects of Music Sociology*. Trans. D. Marinelli. Portland, OR: Amadeus Press, 1992.
A classic in the sociology of music.

Francis Sparshott. *The Future of Aesthetics*. Toronto: University of Toronto Press, 1998.
Philosophical musings on the future relevance of traditional aesthetics.

Jacques Rancière. *Aesthetics and Its Discontents*. Cambridge: Polity Press, 2009.
A postmodern study of the discourse of aesthetics, its colonizing and political discourse, and the resentment it elicits among those who don't accept its totalizing discourse.

Patrick Slattery. *Curriculum Development in the Postmodern Era*. New York: Garland, 1995.
An examination of recent curriculum theory, as informed by postmodernism.

J. M. Bernstein. *The Fate of Art: Aesthetic Alienation from Kant to Derrida and Adorno*. Philadelphia: Pennsylvania State University Press, 1992.
*A critique of "memorial aesthetics" (neo-Kantian), "pure beauty," the "sublime," and an important prediction of the "disintegration" of speculative-rationalist aesthetics. **N.B.**: Since 1992, this disintegration has already happened!*

John Carey. *What Good Are the Arts?* London: Faber and Faber, 2005.
An absorbing study of "is 'high' art superior?"; "Do the arts make us better?"; "Can art be a religion?"; and other penetrating questions.

Joe L. Kincheloe. *Critical Pedagogy*, 2nd ed. New York: Peter Lang, 2009.
Perhaps 'the' most important study of Critical Theory as applied to curriculum; on the need for teachers to engage in ideology critique concerning what and how they teach. An eye-opener as regards curriculum studies.

Thomas A. Regelski and J. Terry Gates, eds. *Music Education for Changing Times: Guiding Vision for Practice*. New York: Springer, 2009.
A selection of seventeen scholarly papers based on praxialism (i.e., focused on the Action Ideals of the MayDay Group, http://www.maydaygroup.org/), with two authors addressing each ideal from different perspectives.

INDEX

Key subjects mentioned in the titles and annotations of the related readings are also indexed.

Made in the USA
Las Vegas, NV
23 November 2021

35170003R00079